MoRe Than WoRdS

FOR KIdS

LeaRn, LoVe, and LiVe by The BiBLe

Mindi Jo Furby

I0149640

HOLY BIBLE

First published April 2014

ISBN: 978-0-9893098-4-4

Visit us on the web!
www.MJFPublishing.com

MJF Publishing exists to fight biblical illiteracy in the church and world. Our goal is to help others love God and become more like Jesus through His Word. We accomplish this through publishing books, articles, curriculum, and Bible studies that educate people about the Bible and inspire them to grow in their relationships with God.

Printed in the United States of America

Published by: MJF Publishing
Edited by: Christina Miller
Illustrations by: Tina Modugno

"Mindi Jo Furby advances her fight against biblical illiteracy with an excellent resource for children, *More than Words for Kids*. Full of engaging illustrations and stories, this book will captivate the hearts of young readers for God and His Word."

Dr. Elmer Towns
Co-Founder, Liberty University
Lynchburg, VA

"Mindi Jo Furby has the unique gift of taking concepts and ideas which can be overwhelming and daunting and putting them into easy-to-grasp themes. She has successfully accomplished this with her book for adults, *More Than Words*, and she has hit it out of the park again with this children's edition. Her use of language will keep adults and children engrossed. Nothing is more important for Christian parents than teaching their children an abiding love for God's Word. And what better way than by teaching our little ones how to study it? Mindi Jo provides a gift to all parents and grandparents everywhere with *More Than Words For Kids*."

Jeff Cranston
Lead Pastor, LowCountry Community Church
Bluffton, SC

"Almost as far back as I can remember, I was exposed to God's Word because of the influence of my mother. However, I also remember my childhood struggle of trying to make sense of some difficult passages and portions of Scripture. Had I only been taught the basic components of how to study the Bible as Mindi Jo Furby has detailed so clearly in *More Than Words For Kids*, most of my challenges would have been resolved. I highly recommend this book as a valuable training tool in the lives of children. It wonderfully explains the treasures found in God's letter to us, but also gives practical helps for children as they begin to study and apply God's truth for themselves!"

Brooks Cail
Senior Pastor, First Baptist Church of the Islands
Savannah, GA

"*More Than Words for Kids* will add spiritual value to anyone at any age. It is important for my wife and me to "Train up our children in the way they should go." I'm the father of a six-year-old and four-year-old, and it did my heart well to see them light up as they read Mindi Jo's words and developed a heart for "God's Special Book," as my kids like to say. My four-year-old loved acting out the word pictures as I read, and my six-year-old especially loved answering the questions at the end of the chapters."

Brian Moore
Lead Pastor, Crosspointe Church
Yorba Linda, CA

"Before the carpenter builds his first home, he must learn the proper use of his tools. This ensures his work will be functional and durable. With *More Than Words For Kids,* Mindi Jo Furby gives children the instruction they need to use the most valuable tool they will ever own: the Bible. With this knowledge, our little ones will be able to use God's Word to build lives for themselves as disciples of Christ with an eternal future."

Marlene Dean
Director of Children's Ministries, Christ Community Church
Pinehurst, NC

"Mindi Jo has created a wonderful one-of-a-kind gift for a very important part of our world: the "tween." As the standards of the world press in on them, she has provided a Biblically sound resource specifically for them. This book will allow and encourage kids to dig deeper into God's Word on their own. They will be encouraged to be joyful, independent students, an important life skill. Parents, Sunday school teachers, and youth leaders will find this a valuable addition to their libraries. Three of my own "tween" grandchildren will be getting a copy."

Sherry Goebel
Mother, Grandmother, Teacher for over twenty-five years
Savannah, GA

"More than Words for Kids is an invaluable resource for parents wanting to help their children understand how we got the Bible we hold in our hands today and how to read it correctly. Mindi Jo Furby has a gift for explaining difficult concepts like *inerrancy* and *hermeneutics* with clarity and excitement. Her passion for God's Word is contagious and jumps out at you with every turn of the page. From wonderful illustrations to practical down-to-earth stories, *More than Words for Kids* is full of Biblical truth that will grow your child's heart closer to God and His Word."

Belinda Furby
Mother, Women's Ministry Bible Study Coordinator
Christ Community Church
Pinehurst, NC

"Mindi has taken complex truth and broken it down to simple, bite-size pieces for children to understand. One of the best kids' books I've read!"

Carie Cash
Children's Pastor, Crosspointe Church
Yorba Linda, CA

"In *More than Words for Kids*, Mindi Jo Furby takes complicated biblical concepts and jargon and transforms them into exciting topics that come alive throughout the text. From her conversational tone to her use of captivating stories, Mindi manages to paint a crystal-clear picture of the Bible's origins and how it should be studied. I wish I'd had this tool as a kid! Even as an adult, I found it to be an excellent and fun refresher course! If God ever blesses me with children, I will certainly use *More than Words for Kids* as a tool to help them discover what it means to study the Bible."

Kaci Hollingsworth
Bachelor of Arts in Sociology, University of NC Chapel Hill
Master of Arts in Teaching Special Education, Armstrong Atlantic State University
Savannah, GA

"We LOOOOOOOOOVE the book and think it is simply AMAZING! Mindi Jo Furby tells stories in the beginning of the chapters, which makes it easier to understand. The way she writes is very easy to read and intriguing. We really enjoyed reading it and think it'll be a big hit! We hope we get a copy before they sell out!"

Elizabeth and Emilee Rinderknecht
Twin sisters, twelve years old
Savannah, GA

Table of Contents

Introduction

Would you like to know something amazing? The most powerful super-hero tool is in your house right now. You might even have one in your room!

It's not a normal tool like the hammer and screwdriver your dad uses. It's also not a magic wand or a special force available only to certain people.

But it is the most powerful tool that exists. No super hero can come close to this tool's power!

Want to know where to find it? Here's a clue: it might be on a bookshelf. That may sound strange, but that's what's cool about this tool — it seems so ordinary that most people overlook it.

They look right past it and miss out on the greatest adventure of their lives. They never realize the power at their fingertips, so they never experience what this tool has to offer.

Well, not you. Not anymore.

Get ready to meet the most supreme tool in the whole universe. It's called *The Bible*.

It seems strange that a *book* would be powerful, but it is. It is so supreme and strong that people have come to life by reading it.

It's so mighty that people risk their lives every day just to read its pages.

Can you imagine risking your life for anything, much less a book?

Well, that's what happens around the world every day. The people who realize the Bible's power are willing to do *anything* to experience the life it offers.

But how is a book powerful? How do a bunch of words make people give up everything and live differently?

That's what this book is all about, and reading it will launch you on the adventure of a lifetime!

The Breakdown

Let's glance at an overview of our adventure before we begin. There are four sections in this book, and each one will focus on a different aspect (part) of the Bible and how we can use it to its fullest potential.

Section One is all *about* the Bible—what it is and why it is the most amazing tool you're ever going to own.

We're going to talk a lot about its characteristics—interesting facts about the Bible. Did you know that the Bible doesn't have any mistakes? Or that it's impossible for it to lie? How about that it's alive? Or that it was written by God Himself?

You're going to discover all those things and more in this section. You'll find out just how incredible this book is, and you might get pretty excited when reading about it!

Section Two is fun because we'll learn where the Bible came from! Have you ever wondered how the Bible was put together or who wrote it? You won't wonder any longer after reading Section Two!

Section Three will give you a chance to make a decision about the Bible and about God. See, it's not enough to know *about* God and the Bible. We need to know God *personally* in order for the Bible to make any difference in our lives. This section will tell you exactly how to do that so you can use your very own super-hero tool as much as possible!

The last section, Section Four, will teach you how to use the Bible. You learn the "secret codes" for reading and understanding the Bible like you never have before. Basically, you'll learn use the Bible as you would a hammer or a saw. You must understand certain things about a tool (and how it works) in order for it to work well. This section will teach you how to use the Bible properly for the best results.

After Section Four, we'll wrap up our time together. Get ready to explore the tool that's more powerful than all the super heroes combined. It's our pleasure to introduce you to…the Bible.

SECTION ONE: What IS the BIBLE?

NO MISTAKES! (INERRANT)

The Perfect Game — Impossible

What do you like to do for fun? Go swimming, ride your bike, draw, play video games? What about sports? Few things in life are more fun than sports…especially sports like soccer.

In soccer, you can run a ball up a field as fast as you can, perform awesome tricks you learn in practice, head the ball back toward the goal, and score points by kicking it right past the goalie's head! Parents cheer, friends give high-fives, and you can become an instant hero with just one goal.

Can you imagine playing a perfect soccer game? The perfect game is more than scoring goals when the other team doesn't. It's a game in which none of your teammates made any mistakes. You scored every time you got the ball, no one ever stole it from you, and you never tripped or fell. In this game, absolutely zero mistakes were made.

How would you like to be on the first team in history to play a perfect game? You'd be hailed (lifted up) as a hero and be interviewed by ESPN! Everyone would want your autograph, and people all around the world would want to be your friend.

It'd be pretty awesome, wouldn't it? All your practice and effort would be worth it to play a perfect game.

Unfortunately, a perfect soccer game is not possible. As long as soccer is around, it will be played by humans (though a chimpanzee soccer game would be pretty funny to watch, wouldn't it?).

But no human is perfect. Even when we try our hardest, we always make a mistake or two. That's why it's impossible to play a perfect game. Because we're not perfect, we can't do anything absolutely perfectly — even play a perfect soccer game.

The Perfect Book — Possible

Did you know that God is perfect? He never makes a mistake or does anything wrong. But what's even more fantastic is that He can't do anything wrong! He is 100 percent perfect all day, every day.

Since God (who's perfect) wrote the Bible, the Bible must be perfect. A perfect God cannot write an imperfect book.

Why Do We Need a Perfect Book?

You may already know this, but God created this world. Though He was perfect and complete in every way, He decided to create a world full of people so He could love them and invite them to love Him back.

But soon He was faced with a problem. The people He created didn't love Him anymore. They decided to live their own way by sinning (disobeying or rebelling) against God. In doing this, they cut off their relationship with Him.

When they realized what they did, they felt terrible. But it was too late. They couldn't do anything to fix it.

It's kind of like losing the ball in soccer. You run as fast as you can and are almost to the goal when someone from the opposing team steals it away from you. Once this happens, it's impossible to undo. Once you lose the ball, the game moves on and there's nothing you can do about it.

You can't rewind the game or start it over.

That's what happened with people after they sinned. They couldn't go back and fix it, so they cried out to God for help. They knew that because God is perfect, He could help them make things right and heal the relationship between them.

But the healing process was a long one.

Have you ever been hurt before? Perhaps you've broken your arm or had your tonsils taken out. Whenever we get really hurt, it takes a long time for us to heal. Our bodies have to fix what was broken, and we can't do anything to make it happen faster. All we can do is listen to and obey our doctor and parents, and wait for our injury to heal.

That's exactly how it was with the sin problem people created. People caused great pain to themselves and to God, and though He began healing them immediately, the process took time.

But He didn't leave us alone to heal by ourselves. He gave us the greatest healing tool we could ever have imagined. He gave us something that would help us go through the healing process and make the best of a bad situation.

He gave us the tool we talked about earlier…the Bible.

The Bible is a book God gave us to tell us how He, His Son, Jesus, and His Holy Spirit would help us get back into a relationship (connection) with Him.

No other book or person or letter or song shows us God like the Bible does, because the Bible is God's words written down for us to read.

That's pretty AMAZING when you think about it, isn't it?!

God, who is absolutely perfect, knew we needed the perfect tool to heal us—to make us more like Him. So He decided to give it to us in the form of a book—a perfect book that doesn't have a single, itty-bitty mistake anywhere in it.

That's the first characteristic we'll learn about the Bible—that it doesn't have a single mistake.

It's For Real!

Do you have a Bible? Do you know where it is? The Bible is to books what a perfect soccer game is to soccer (except it's real, of course). It contains zero mistakes.

Every letter, word, and punctuation mark in the Bible (when it was originally or first written) is correct and in its proper place. Not only that, everything it says is true! It's a real-life hero— absolutely perfect, 100 percent true, and very powerful—just like God, who wrote it.

There's a fancy word for this. Get ready to impress your friends! If something doesn't have any mistakes and is completely true, it's called *inerrant*. Inerrant simply means "without error."

The Bible, like the universe, was absolutely perfect when it was written down. But unlike the universe, which is degenerating (falling apart) daily, the Bible has remained strong and is as powerful today as it was when it was written.

Let's go back in time for a minute to imagine how the world was when the Bible was written down for the first time.

A Long, Long Time Ago

The Bible was written a long time ago—a *really, really, really, really, really* long time ago. Do you think your grandparents are old? Just imagine how old their grandparents would be if they were still alive. Then imagine how old their grandparents would be. You get the picture.

We have to go way back in time to see how old the Bible is because it was written over 2,000 years ago.

In those days, people didn't have computers, iPads, or Kindles. They didn't even have pens or notebook paper. They had to make their own writing utensils out of feathers and paper from plants. Think about having to cut down a tree every time you wanted to write something down. That'd be pretty annoying!

Well, that's how people had to do it back then. God chose a very small group of people to write down His perfect words, and they used feather pens and parchment scrolls to do it. (See the picture.) These writings were 100 percent true—completely inerrant.

God Kept Writing

Because God is amazing, He didn't give us just a small letter to read. He gave us hundreds of chapters and dozens of books—all put into one big book. As God's chosen people kept writing His words, the scrolls got bigger and bigger. Before long, people had to start making copies of the scrolls (books) so everyone could read them.

How Did They Do It?

Along with an absence of laptops, there were also no copiers in those days. People couldn't just go to a store and have something copied for them. They had to hand-write every single letter, word, and punctuation mark to make copies of the writings.

Can you imagine copying something as big as the Bible word for word? That would be so hard! And it would take forever!

It *was* hard. But these people, known as scribes, dedicated their lives to copying Scripture. Their job was to copy each scroll of the Bible word for word, and they did it all day long—almost every day—for years and years.

The Big Question

> *Since humans aren't perfect, how did human scribes copy the Bible so it stayed perfect?*

When Scripture was first written down, it was absolutely perfect because it came straight from God, who is perfect. Scribes were then given the task of copying each word of the original scrolls. They were supposed to preserve (keep) them as perfectly as possible, as close to the original scrolls as they could.

They took this job very seriously.

Because they knew that the Bible came from God, they were very careful in writing it down and making copies. They were so careful, in fact, that if they made just one mistake (due to being human and not perfect), they would destroy the entire scroll!

Can you imagine writing out an entire page of homework and then throwing the whole thing away because you made one little mistake?

That's what the scribes did. Since God is perfect and He gave them a perfect book, it was their job to keep it as perfect as possible.

It was a difficult and time-consuming process. But God told them to do it, and they obeyed Him with all their hearts.

A Few Bumps in the Road

The Bibles we have in our houses today exist only because the scribes were so careful with their copying duties. God preserved His Word faithfully and carefully from ancient times until now.

But because humans aren't perfect, a couple of tiny mistakes have crept their way into the translated Bibles we have today.

Here's another big-word phrase for you to impress your friends with: *textual discrepancies* (text-u-all dis-krep-in-sees). Textual discrepancies are basically the tiny mistakes that have made their way into our English Bibles today.

But I thought the Bible was inerrant (mistake-free). It was — when it was originally written. But since then, itty-bitty mistakes got into the Bible when it was copied and translated over thousands of years.

The important point to note about these discrepancies, though, is that not a single one compromises (casts doubt on) God's truth or promises in the Bible.

Every hiccup found in our copies of the Bible affects only the language of how the Bible is written, not the truth the languages are communicating.

Let's say it an easier way.

The discrepancies are found in *how* it's said, not *what* is said.

Here's a make-believe example:

- Let's say the original scroll for Genesis 1:1 says…

  "In the beginning, God created the heavens and the earth."

- And the copies we have today for Genesis 1:1 say…

  "In the <u>very</u> beginning, God created the heavens and the earth."

What is this verse saying? That's right — God created the heavens and the earth in the beginning of time.

Do you see the difference between the two examples above? The second example added the word "very" to the original example, which makes it different than the original one.

But does this textual discrepancy change what the verse is saying? Not at all! The point of the verse is still being taught to us, even though there is a minor difference in the second example as compared to the first one.

That's what we mean by the "errors" in our Bibles today being simple textual discrepancies. A couple of "mistakes" have crept into the Bible after being copied and translated for years and years, but none of them change what God is saying through the words.

So the Bibles we have today are still inerrant in the promises and truth it talks about. God preserved His truth and kept it entirely inerrant, despite the fact that non-perfect people copied it for years and years.

God would never let His Bible get a real mistake in it (one that compromises His truth). He is too perfect and His Word is too important for it to be compromised.

The Bible is how God has chosen to speak to us. How amazing that He's kept it so close to its original perfection all these years so we never have to doubt it—or Him.

It's pretty fantastic! Now that we know all about inerrancy, let's talk about the Bible's next characteristic: infallibility.

Make It YOURS!

- What does inerrant mean?

- Who copied each page of the Bible before computers and printers existed?

- Why is the Bible trustworthy?

2

NO LIES! (INFALLIBLE)

Tracy loves animals—every type of animal, big or small. Her parents will let her have only one pet (a puppy named Toby), so she takes care of him as if he is a prince! She feeds him, walks him, and plays fetch with him every day.

Along with taking care of Toby, Tracy also volunteers at the local animal shelter to take care of the neglected animals there. It makes her sad that so many people abuse animals, and she feels she can help by volunteering to take care of them.

Tracy's best friend, Kate, loves animals too. She has two dogs, a black cat, and a chubby bunny. If her parents would let her, she'd rescue every pet she came across. She just can't say no to animals—especially if they've been abandoned or abused!

The good news is that Kate's parents will let her have one more pet. She already has a black kitten named Blacky, and now she's looking for a white kitten. She's been waiting months to find just the right one at the animal shelter, but hasn't found "the one" yet.

One afternoon, while Tracy was feeding the puppies at the animal shelter, the shelter's manager walked into the room, holding the most beautiful little kitten Tracy had ever seen. His coat was as bright as fresh-fallen snow, and his eyes shined like clear blue water.

Tracy fell in love instantly but knew her parents would never let her keep the little kitten. She immediately thought about Kate. This kitten would be Kate's dream come true — the perfect white kitty to go with her black one.

But she didn't want to tell Kate about the kitten. Tracy wanted to keep the kitten for herself, even though she knew her parents wouldn't let her. The thought of watching Kate with the kitten made her squirm with jealously. She determined right then and there that Kate would never hear about the little white kitten.

"So," she thought, "if I can't keep this kitten, then neither should Kate. I'll just keep the kitten a secret so another family will adopt him instead."

Later that week, Tracy found herself in a tricky situation. Kate asked her if any new animals had been brought to the animal shelter.

Tracy froze.

She just couldn't bear the thought of Kate having that kitten! So she lied.

She told Kate that the shelter hadn't received any white kittens, but she'd keep looking for her. Tracy continued lying to Kate for weeks until she heard the kitten had been adopted.

"Whew!" she thought. "Now I don't have to lie to Kate anymore. I'm sure the kitty found a great home and will be very happy."

Tracy thought she got away with it until one dreadful afternoon when Kate stormed into the animal shelter, eyes burning with tears. She raced up to Tracy and said, "Why did you lie to me?"

"What are you talking about?"

"You know *exactly* what I'm talking about!" Kate yelled. "You knew about the little white kitten but didn't tell me about him!"

"What white kitten? There hasn't been a white kitten around here." Tracy continued the lie.

"That's such a lie! My parents surprised me with the kitten last night and told me that he's been at the shelter for weeks, just waiting for the perfect family to adopt him. You're supposed to be my friend!"

Kate stalked away before Tracy could respond. Tracy felt sick about lying to her. She knew that she'd hurt their friendship deeply, maybe even forever. Right then, she promised herself never to hurt anyone like that again.

No Good Lies

Have you ever been lied to like Kate? It's a terrible feeling and it can ruin everything — even friendships. There's nothing worse than being deceived by someone you love. It makes trusting anyone nearly impossible, and the hurt is hard to overcome.

But there's great news if you believe in God and have accepted Jesus as your Savior…

God *never* lies to you. In fact, He's incapable of lying (not able to lie) at all!

How comforting is that? Our perfect God, who gave us His perfect Word, cannot lie to us. He can't deceive us, mislead us, or make us think anything that's not true.

This is a big deal because again, if God can't lie, neither can the Bible! Not only does the Bible not have mistakes, it's not capable of making mistakes!

The big word that describes this characteristic about the Bible is the word *infallible*. Infallible, like inerrancy, means that the Bible doesn't have any mistakes.

But infallibility takes inerrancy a bit further. Instead of simply meaning that the Bible does not make mistakes (inerrancy), infallibility means the Bible cannot make mistakes.

The Bible can't lie to us because God can't lie. He loves us too much to lie to us. He tells us the truth, even if the truth is hard to hear.

We Can Misinterpret (Misunderstand)

Though the Bible cannot lie, we can misinterpret and misunderstand what it says. Remember, we're humans and we make a lot of mistakes!

Sometimes when we read the Bible, we think it says something that it doesn't. Other times, we don't read it correctly or don't pay enough attention to what is written for us.

Regardless, if somebody makes a mistake regarding the Bible, we're the ones making it. We can (and do) make mistakes, but it never does.

Ramifica-what?

Want to learn another awesome word? *Ramifications.* Ramifications are consequences or unavoidable reactions to events. Every cause has an effect.

For example, if you spill a glass of milk on the floor (cause), the ramifications (effects) of that spill include:

1. Having to clean up the mess

2. Buying a new glass because the old one broke

3. Maybe being punished by your parents for not being careful

4. Changing your shirt if any spilled on it

5. Having to pour another glass if you're still thirsty

There are several ramifications (effects) of a spilled glass of milk (cause). Everything that happens in life has ramifications.

Think back to Tracy and Kate's story. Tracy lied to Kate (cause), which had serious ramifications (effects). The ramifications included:

1. Kate's hurt feelings

2. A deeply hurt friendship

3. Distrust between Kate and Tracy

4. Tracy feeling guilty

Again, everything has ramifications, including the Bible and its infallibility.

A Choice We Must Make

If everything the Bible says is true, then we have to make a decision about it. We must decide if we believe it or not.

Our decision (whichever one we make) has lots of ramifications, just like Tracy's choice to lie to Kate did.

If we choose to believe the Bible, we can rest assured that God will strengthen us, comfort us, and fulfill every single one of His promises for us, His children.

If we choose not to believe the Bible and its truth, we won't receive any of the blessings God promises us. The greatest blessing of all is knowing Him personally, but if we refuse to believe the Bible, we'll never know Him and will end up spending all of eternity apart from Him.

He gives us our entire lives to decide which choice we will make. Will we believe that the Bible is truth and enjoy the wonderful life He has for us? Or will we reject the Bible and stay away from Him forever? He gives us a choice and we should be wise in choosing.

The Truth about Truth

One fact to consider in your choice is that truth is truth, whether we believe it or not. Here's an example for you. What color is the sky? Yep! It's blue. But what if someone came up to you and said,

> *"Well, I don't believe the sky is blue. I*
> *think it's red, so from now on, it's red."*

That person would be a little crazy, right? We can't change the color of the sky just because we don't want to believe it's blue. The sky is blue whether we believe it or not!

The same can be said about truth. Truth doesn't change because of what we believe. Truth is always true, whether we believe it or not. And we can't change the truth (God's truth, the Bible) just because we don't like it.

We're held accountable to truth, even if we choose not to believe it. Remember, there are ramifications for our choices. Choosing not to believe God's truth in the Bible is dangerous. If we reject Christ, then we reject His promises, grace, mercy, love, and truth in the Bible. We reject a relationship with Him and will spend forever away from Him.

If God says in the Bible that everyone who doesn't accept Jesus won't go to heaven, they won't go to heaven. They can wish to go to heaven and hope to go to heaven, but if they don't accept Jesus, they won't.

The decision we make now about the Bible and its infallibility has huge ramifications for our future. Will you trust God — that He and His Bible are perfect and don't lie? Or will you reject Him and regret it deeply later on?

The choice is yours. Choose wisely.

Make It YOURS!

- What is the difference between inerrant and infallible?

- What are ramifications?

- Are there ramifications for not believing that the Bible is infallible? If so, what are they?

A Present Just for Us! (Inspired)

Now that we have a grasp of the Bible's inerrancy and infallibility, let's move on to the third characteristic: its inspiration.

What's your favorite holiday? If you live in America, do you love stuffing your face with turkey on Thanksgiving or going to barbeques and picnics on the Fourth of July?

Christmas is a tough one to beat. Who doesn't love sipping hot cocoa, singing carols, decorating the tree, tasting candy canes, and seeing your neighborhood all lit up with sparkling lights?

Does your family have any special Christmas traditions? If not, do you know anyone who does? Do you go caroling as a family? Or perhaps attend a Christmas Eve service at church?

Do you eat a huge breakfast of pancakes and bacon in the morning or help prepare a family feast for dinner?

Regardless of your traditions, Christmas is amazing. Especially the presents.

Opening presents on Christmas morning is one of the greatest experiences in the world. It's the one morning in the year when you want to wake up early!

We get butterflies of excitement in our stomachs as we race out of bed down the hall and straight to the shining tree towering above the sea of presents.

It's tough to be patient on Christmas morning, isn't it? We can't wait to demolish the bows, ribbons, and paper to see the presents beneath them.

Families are full of smiles and joy as each gift is opened. We hug each other as our faces beam with sheer delight.

It's a glorious day indeed.

The Greatest Gift-Giver

Would it surprise you to know that God loves giving us gifts? Seriously! He loves giving us presents and surprise blessings whenever He can.

This may also surprise you: He's already given you the best present you've ever received. Yep. Even better than the bike, the best video game, the newest technological gadget, and the pony — if you're that lucky.

The first gift He gave us is the reason we celebrate Christmas at all — Jesus. Jesus was more than a good guy who did lots of cool things. He's not just a good teacher and kind person. Nor is He only a man who started a popular religion.

Jesus is God. He is so important that even His proper pronouns are capitalized. (We use "He" instead of "he" when we write about God, Jesus, and the Holy Spirit because He's God!) Jesus came to earth as a man to give us the greatest gift we could ever imagine: hope.

We all know that there's more to life than what we see with our eyes on earth. Like we mentioned before, we go somewhere when we die; we don't just disappear. The Bible says that we go one of two places — with God in heaven or without Him in hell. In heaven, we'll be with God forever; in hell, people will spend eternity in utter pain and fear apart from Him.

Jesus came to make a way for us to spend forever with God. We can choose God and joy that lasts forever, or we can choose ourselves and spend forever apart from Him.

You don't need to be a genius to guess which choice is better!

Yet many people choose the wrong one. They trust themselves over God; they choose hell instead of heaven; they believe lies instead of truth.

This often happens because people don't know about the gift. Oh, they may hear about it from their friends or pastors, but in the end, they don't know enough to make a wise decision about Jesus. They never realize how great a gift He is, and they miss out on everything He offers them.

Fortunately, God knew this would happen. Long before He created the world, He knew some people would remain stubborn and not want to obey Him. Some would refuse the precious gift He offers them.

But He also knew that some people would want to be close to Him. Some would want to be in a personal relationship with Him, like a father and son or best friends are.

Since He loves everyone the same (whether or not they love Him back), He decided to give the world another gift.

Though the second gift isn't as magnificent as Jesus, we wouldn't know very much about Jesus without it. Can you guess what it is?

The Bible!

The third characteristic of the Bible is that it is an inspired gift, just for us. Without the Bible, we wouldn't know anything about Jesus, why He came, or how we can accept Him as our Savior and be in a relationship with God.

Without the Bible, we wouldn't know about faith, truth, or what to believe in. We wouldn't know that God created the world, nor would we be assured that we could go to heaven with Him one day.

Basically, we wouldn't know very much at all about God without the Bible!

That's why it's such a precious gift. Sure, it's great that it doesn't have any errors and it can't lie to us. But it doesn't do much good for us until we realize what an amazing gift it is.

Two Reasons

The Bible is a great gift for two reasons:

1. Because God gave it to us

2. Because we didn't (don't) deserve it

As we said earlier, God created the entire universe and everything in it...including you! When you go outside and see trees, animals, the sun and clouds, you know God made each and every one of them.

When you laugh and play with your family and friends, you know God created every one of them too.

God is creative and designed this entire world with us in mind. He created plants, animals, oceans, deserts, and lakes for us to enjoy. He's given us everything we could possibly need... including life itself.

Yet He didn't stop at giving us what we need physically (just for our bodies). He went a step further and gave us what we need spiritually (for our souls that last forever and ever) so we can know Him and love Him back.

On top of everything He's already given us, He gives us the Bible. He took the time to write and preserve the Bible so we can get to know Him. He carefully kept it around just for us so we could read it and learn all about what He's doing in the world.

The Bible is an astonishing gift of love straight from God. He didn't have to give it to us, but He still did—for our benefit. He knows we're most happy when we're in a growing relationship with Him, and the Bible helps us get there.

The second reason the Bible is a great gift is because we don't deserve it. Imagine giving a present to your little brother, who just got on your nerves and was acting dumb.

You wouldn't really want to give him a present, right?

Well, that's exactly how our relationship with God is when He gives us the Bible. We don't always have a wonderful relationship with Him. Sometimes we get mad at Him. Other times we ignore Him, and sometimes we disobey Him without saying we're sorry.

Yet God loves us so much that He still gives us gifts—specifically the gift of the Bible. The Bible is from God. It's not a book that a bunch of silly people made up in their imaginations. It's God's words to us and for us so we can be in a good and growing relationship with Him—the King of the universe!

How It Got from God to Us

If the Bible is from God, did He write it down Himself? Nope. Though every single word came from Him, He used people to write down His words.

Basically, He told the people what to write, and they wrote it down exactly as He said. He gave some people dreams about what to write, and He spoke directly to others about what to write.

The exact way God gave the writers instructions was special to each writer. He doesn't always tell us how He told them what to write. But what really matters is the fact that He did tell them.

This is called *inspiration.* Inspiration means that God inspired (or caused) people to write down His words exactly as He wanted.

How did God tell the writers what to write without saying it to them out loud? Though God doesn't tell us exactly, I bet you do this with your mom and dad sometimes.

If you're not allowed to snack on cookies before dinner, and your mom hears you opening the cookie jar and looks at you, she doesn't have to say anything for you to know she caught you, right? You know exactly what she's thinking, even though she doesn't say a word. She wants you out of that cookie jar now!

At this point, you're very inspired to get your hand out of that jar before she gets you in trouble! And if someone asked you to write down her silent words, you'd probably answer something like,

> *"Son, get your hand out of that cookie jar right this minute! You'll ruin your appetite for dinner if you don't!"*

Just like you know what your mom would say because you know her well, sometimes the writers of the Bible knew what God was saying because they knew Him well. They were close to Him and often knew what He wanted to write, just as you sometimes know what your mom wants you to do.

God would not allow one letter or word to be written in His book if it was not what He wanted. So He made sure the people He chose for the task obeyed Him very closely.

Put yourself in their position for a minute. Wouldn't it be scary to write down the very words of God? You bet it would be! Yet God helped them through the process, just as He helps us when we need it today.

The Bible is a precious gift to us because it came straight from God when we didn't deserve it. Though He used people to write it down on scrolls, every single letter, line, and punctuation mark was written exactly as He wanted.

Take a minute today and just hold your Bible. Think about what an awesome gift it is from God Himself—far more powerful, spectacular, and unstoppable than any superhero you could ever imagine.

MAKE IT YOURS!

- Why is the Bible a GREAT gift?

- How did God choose to write down the words of the Bible?

- Do we deserve a gift like the Bible? Why or why not?

It's Alive! (Living)

You've learned many cool words about the Bible already! You've learned:

1. Inerrant

2. Infallible

3. Inspired

...and we've only just begun! If you weren't a Bible genius before you started this book, you're well on your way now.

The fourth characteristic of the Bible doesn't have a special big word, but it's totally awesome anyway. This characteristic is that the Bible is alive.

Camping Mishap

James and Ricky love camping. They've been best friends since they were little and go camping with their dads every summer.

Some nights, their parents even let them camp out in the backyard. They pitch their tent, roast marshmallows over the fire, and feast on gooey s'mores. They tell each other scary stories and make funny faces with their flashlights before drifting off to sleep. It's every boy's dream!

One day, Ricky's dad showed up at their school completely unexpected. He signed Ricky and James out of class and started walking with them to the car.

James and Ricky pestered him with questions about where they were going, and when Ricky's dad couldn't take it anymore, he announced with a twinkle in his eye…

"We're going camping, boys!"

"Right now?"

"Yep! James' dad is waiting for us at home. We're already packed! What do you think about playing hooky from school to go camping?"

Needless to say, the boys were thrilled! Missing school and going camping with their dads — a perfect combination.

After a long but fun drive of listening to music, laughing, and telling stories, they finally arrived. They each grabbed their gear and started their mile-long hike to their favorite campsite near the swampy marshes along the river.

But on their way something happened. James dropped his compass on the side of the trail. As he reached down to get it, he saw the coolest-looking plant he'd ever seen!

It looked like a weird taco shell. It was green on the outside, pink on the inside, and had wispy finger-looking things around the edges.

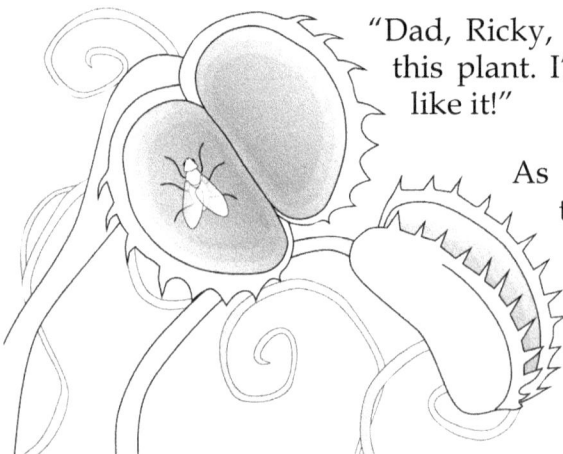

"Dad, Ricky, Mr. Matt, come look at this plant. I've never seen anything like it!"

As the guys came around to see what James was talking about, James inched in closer and closer to get a better look. Apparently, a fly

26

was mesmerized by the plant too, because it landed right on the middle of it.

James got closer and closer until all of a sudden…

SNAP!

The plant snapped shut and ate the fly!!! James was so scared he fell backwards and cried, "Ah!"

Ricky and the dads ran over quickly and helped James stand up again. When they asked what happened, James yelled, "The plant ate a fly! It was just sitting there all still and it came to life and ate a bug!"

Ricky's eyes got as big as lemons. He couldn't believe it! But the dads could. They looked at each other and smiled. Then they told James and Ricky that the plant was called a Venus flytrap. It was alive and ate insects.

What James thought was an ordinary plant was actually very alive and moved quicker than a ninja!

Very Much Alive

So far we've seen how the Bible…

1. Doesn't have mistakes

2. Can't make mistakes or lie

3. Is an inspired gift straight from God to us

Now we get to see something that sounds as strange as a Venus flytrap: the Bible is alive!

No, the Bible doesn't breathe or grow feet so it can walk around. It also doesn't eat bugs, although you could probably swat a bug with it. But it does speak to us exactly when and how we need it to.

God doesn't usually communicate with us by speaking to us out loud as people do. But if we believe and follow Jesus, He does give us His Holy Spirit to speak to us through the pages of His Word.

Some people think the Bible doesn't have anything to say for us today. They think that because it was written a long time ago, it can't give us any direction in our modern lives.

If the Bible was like any other book, they'd be correct. But because it's unique — because it's alive — they couldn't be more wrong.

Though it was written a long time ago, it doesn't make sense or apply only to people living back then. God talks to us today through the very words He wrote thousands of years ago.

When we read the Bible, God teaches us how we can best follow Him and make good choices. For example, pretend there's a new kid at school named Chanel, who doesn't have any friends because she dresses differently than everyone else. Some of your friends won't be her friend because of her clothes, and now you have to decide if you're going to be friends with her.

If you read the Bible, you'll discover how Jesus loved everyone — even those who were viewed as different by people in society. Some people known as Pharisees (fair-uh-sees) looked down on people who weren't like them. They were mean to them and treated them very poorly.

Well, Jesus wasn't like the Pharisees at all. Instead of being mean to people who were different, He embraced them and loved them.

That gives you the answer of what you should do about Chanel. If Jesus loved everyone and treated everyone with kindness, then we should too. People who weren't treated well by the Pharisees loved Jesus because He made them feel special. Can you imagine how good Chanel would feel if you invited her to eat lunch with you or walked with her to class?

She'd probably appreciate it a lot.

See, the Bible is alive. God uses it to "tell" us what to do when we're stuck about a decision. His Holy Spirit (who lives in our hearts) guides us to make choices that will make us more like Jesus.

The Holy Spirit

We'll never understand how the Bible is alive until we understand the Holy Spirit.

Have you heard of the Holy Spirit? He is the third member of the Trinity (God). God is three persons in one. The three are: God the Father, God the Son (Jesus Christ), and God the Holy Spirit.

It's difficult to understand how God is three in one, but think of it like an egg. One egg has three parts:

1. The shell

2. The yolk (yellow part)

3. The egg white (white part)

It's still only one egg, but it has three parts.

God is similar to that and we refer to Him as the Trinity. Each member of the Trinity has a specific function or role to play. God the Father plans things for the universe and for His children (us). God the Son (Jesus) carries out the Father's will—He came and died for us and fights for us daily against the devil. God the Holy Spirit is with us all day, every day to help us grow in our relationships with God.

A Person

It's important to understand that the Holy Spirit is a being like a person. A lot of people mistakenly believe that He is a ghost or force or beam of light that swirls mystically around us. That's simply not true!

The Holy Spirit is just as much a personal being as God the Father and Jesus Christ. He has feelings and emotions, makes decisions, and has a job to do. He's not a phantom, ghost, or spirit that floats around the atmosphere. He's a very personal being, and Someone we can get to know very well.

He's God

Just like it's important to understand the Holy Spirit is a being, we must also remember that He is God. We can pray to Him, worship Him, obey Him, and love Him, just as we do the other two members of the Trinity.

The Holy Spirit isn't understood as well as God the Father or Jesus, but that doesn't mean He is any less God. He is 100 percent perfect and holy. He never makes mistakes, and He cannot lie. He loves us deeply and works day and night to bring us closer to God.

He Helps Us

How does the Holy Spirit help us? First of all, He's always with us. As soon as we accept Jesus as our Savior, God gives us the Holy Spirit to be with us all day, every day, for the rest of our lives (Ephesians 1:13-14).

He comes to live with us and in our hearts. He also never leaves us, and He loves us a lot. But being with us isn't the only thing He cares about. He also wants us to "grow up" in Jesus.

Have you ever seen a newborn baby? Maybe you have a little brother or sister you remember seeing for the first time when he or she was born. Babies are very small and can't do anything for themselves. Someone else (usually their parents) has to feed them, wash them, clothe them, and change their diapers.

But as they grow, things change. They are slowly able to do things for themselves, like eating on their own and putting on their own clothes. Before too long, they're eating "normal" food (not the mushy baby stuff), talking, and learning new things.

We've all grown from being a helpless baby. It's called life. We start very small and grow in every way — physically (our bodies), emotionally (our feelings), and spiritually (with God).

Our relationships with Jesus are much the same as our growth from babies to adults. When we accept Jesus into our hearts, we are little "babies" in our faith (spiritually). We don't know very much, and we need God and others to teach us how to follow Him.

But as we learn and get to know Jesus more, we "grow up" and become more like Him. That's the whole point of being a Christian — to look and be more like Jesus (Hebrews 5:12-14).

The Holy Spirit uses the Bible to help us "grow up" in Jesus. He doesn't want us staying babies forever and ever. If we're honest, we don't want to stay babies either.

From the moment Jesus becomes the King in our lives, the Holy Spirit begins working to make us strong and grown up in our faith. He teaches us the Bible and helps us understand what it says so we can be like Jesus.

What He Does Not Do

The Holy Spirit helps us a lot. In fact, we cannot become like Jesus at all without Him. But there are some things He doesn't do. Though He helps us read the Bible, He doesn't do everything for us.

1. **The Holy Spirit does not make us understand the Bible perfectly every time we read it.**

As we've learned, the Bible is inerrant and infallible. It has no mistakes, nor can it make mistakes. The Bible is absolutely perfect…but we are not.

Sometimes we make mistakes and misunderstand things— even the Bible. Though the Holy Spirit helps us understand the Bible, He doesn't read it for us. Nor does He magically make us understand it perfectly the first time we read it.

Like everything else in life, sometimes we have to work hard to learn. There will be times when you read the Bible and have a hard time understanding what it says. But because we have the Holy Spirit, when we get stuck, all we have to do is pray and ask Him for help. He may help you directly (just you, Him, and the Bible), or He might send someone else to help you understand. We can always trust that He'll help us, but that doesn't mean we can be lazy.

2. **The Holy Spirit does not create new meaning in the Bible.**

As soon as John (one of Jesus' followers) finished writing Revelation (the last book in the Bible), the Bible was complete. No one else can add to it. No one can take anything away from it.

The Bible is perfectly complete. But some people try to add or take things away from it, claiming "The Holy Spirit told me so!"

If someone claims the Holy Spirit told them about a new truth that's not in the Bible, they are not telling the truth (Revelation 22:18-19).

God wrote everything He wanted to write in the Bible, and it's perfect just the way it is. The Holy Spirit helps us understand the truth He already revealed. He doesn't add or subtract anything from it.

3. The Holy Spirit does not change the Bible to make it say what we want it to say.

Sometimes we wish we didn't have to do what our parents tell us. We don't like making our beds or brushing our teeth or eating vegetables. If we're honest, we must admit that sometimes we lie to get out of doing something.

Pretend your mom says you have to finish your vegetables before you can have ice cream. Instead of eating them yourself, you give them to your dog when Mom's not looking.

Even though the vegetables are gone, you did not obey your mom, did you?

Sometimes we do that with the Bible. If the Bible tells us to obey our parents, but we don't feel like it, sometimes we ignore it or pretend it says something else. The Holy Spirit does not change the Bible to make it say what we want it to. He doesn't let us interpret the Bible however we want. Instead, He helps us understand it as God meant it when He wrote it.

The Holy Spirit keeps the Bible alive. Many people think the Bible is stagnant (like James mistakenly thought the Venus flytrap was), but we've seen how untrue that is. The Bible is vibrant and alive. The Holy Spirit uses it to grow us into followers of Jesus who look, talk, and are like Him.

MaKe It YOURS!

- How is the Bible *alive*?

- How does God speak to us today through the Bible?

- Who is the Holy Spirit? How does He help us read and understand the Bible?

5

What A Story (Word Of God)

The Bible is alive, perfect, incapable of telling lies, and inspired by God Himself. That's a lot of wonderful characteristics! Before we move on to the next section, we have one last trait to discover: the Bible is a *story*.

A Part of the Story

Who's your favorite character or super hero? Maybe it's Superman. Or, for girls, it could be a Disney princess. We each have a hero or someone we look up to. Sometimes we even wish we could be them!

Part of what makes our heroes and favorite characters so great is their stories. Superman goes on awesome adventures! Wouldn't it be cool to be him for just one day? You could fly, fight bad guys, and help people in need!

For girls, it would be dazzling to be a princess, wouldn't it? You could wear the most beautiful clothes, do whatever you wanted, and be loved by all the princes around. Sounds pretty amazing!

Our favorite characters have stories we love and want to be a part of. Imagine if you could be part of a fantastic story. What would it be like to be a character in a great adventure like the ones we watch in movies or read about in books? That would be something we'd remember forever and ever, wouldn't it?

If you agree, there's great news for you. You are part of an amazing story, even if you don't know it. And the best part is that this story is better than any superhero or princess story that's ever been told!

One Big Story

Though the Bible has lots of books and tons of stories, it all makes up one big story. This story is called the gospel, and it's something you are a part of.

The "gospel" is a fancy word for "good news." Have you heard your pastor or teachers talk about the gospel before? It's the best story we could ever imagine.

> *In short, the gospel is the story of how God saves people, making a way for them to be with Him forever and ever.*

The Bad Guy of the Story

We talked about it a little bit before, but we are cursed by something called sin.

Sin is anything we do that God doesn't like. God is good and perfect and wants us to be like Him. When we love each other, are nice to our brothers and sisters, and share with our friends, God smiles because we are being like Him.

But when we tell a lie, take something that's not ours, or make fun of people, God is not happy. These things are examples of sin—things that aren't good and don't make God happy.

The bad news is that everyone is born a sinner. Every single person does bad things. Some people act worse than others, but the truth is that we all sin and make bad choices (Romans 3:23).

Sin is a lot worse than we think. Of course, it's not good to hurt people's feelings and make mistakes. But the worst part of sin is that it keeps us from being close to God.

In order to understand the big story of the Bible, we first need to understand the reason the story exists at all. Sin is a big part of it, so let's discover where it came from.

Where Sin Came From

Have you ever heard the story of creation? It's the very first story in the Bible, and it tells us how God created the whole world and everything in it. He created the stars, the moon, and the sun. He also created the smallest ant, the biggest elephant, and the funniest-looking fish in the sea (Genesis 1-2).

The best part of the creation story is that God created everything perfect. The weather was always perfect. There were no scary tornadoes or earthquakes or thunderstorms that make us hide under our covers. Every single animal got along with each other. Even tigers and sheep! Every part of the world was perfect and lived in complete harmony — peace with one another.

One day, that all changed. Adam and Eve (the first two humans created) made a big mistake. God told them not to eat from one certain tree, but they disobeyed Him. They ate from the tree God told them not to eat from. They sinned (Genesis 3).

As soon as they sinned, the world wasn't perfect anymore. Animals didn't get along, and in time, weather got worse and storms came around. People no longer treated each other nicely all the time, and life became harder.

Something else happened when Adam and Eve sinned, though. *They were separated from God.* Before they sinned, they were very close to God, but now they found themselves far away from Him.

Who's your best friend in the whole world? You probably spend a lot of time with them and love to do things together. That's how Adam, Eve, and God were before they disobeyed Him. They were together all the time, could talk about anything, and would even go on walks together.

They could do this because they were good, like God. But when they messed up, they could no longer be in that wonderful relationship with Him. God stayed perfect and He couldn't be close to people who weren't.

It's kind of like what happened between Tracy and Kate in chapter two. When Tracy lied to Kate, their friendship got messed up. It couldn't be the same anymore because Kate couldn't trust Tracy.

In a similar way, God and Adam and Eve couldn't be close anymore because Adam and Eve hurt God by sinning against Him. They disobeyed Him, which hurt their relationship with Him deeply.

The Story Begins...and Continues

That story is the beginning of the Bible. God created everything perfectly, but humans messed it up. The rest of the story (and the Bible) is God cleaning up the mess we made.

At the end of the first sin story, God makes a promise. He promises that one day He would come and make everything right (Genesis 3:15). The rest of the Bible is God showing us how He's fulfilling His promise.

Every single part of the Bible points to one person—Jesus Christ. Jesus is God who came to earth as a man to fix what Adam and Eve messed up a long time before He came.

Imagine for a moment that your grandma did something bad a long time ago. Then think what it would be like for God to tell her He'd make it all better…except that He wouldn't do it until you were born. That's a long time to wait!

The world had to wait a long time for Jesus to come, but it was worth the wait! The Bible tells the whole story of how we sinned and how Jesus came to save us.

How He Fixed It

Though Adam and Eve were the first ones to sin, they weren't the last ones to sin. Each of us makes mistakes and does bad things every single day. Have you gotten mad at your brother or sister today? Or did you not tell the whole truth to your mom? If either of those happened, you sinned today.

Everyone sins every single day because everyone is a sinner. Even one tiny sin makes you a sinner. How is that possible?

Well, let's pretend that sin is like blue food coloring. Have you ever used food coloring? If so, then you know that just one tiny drop of blue food coloring will turn a whole bowl of frosting blue.

What if you put a tiny drop of blue food coloring into a jar of beautiful, clear water? Just like with the frosting, the entire jar of water will turn blue. It is the same way with sin. One tiny sin will turn us completely into sinners.

Once the jar of water has been changed to blue with the food coloring, you cannot make it clear again. In the same way, once you have sinned, you cannot do anything to make yourself *not* a sinner.

Jesus, on the other hand, has a jar of clean water. Since Jesus is God, He is perfect. He has never sinned, and He can never sin. He cannot make His own water dirty. He has no sin to drop into his jar.

Jesus' clean water is very good news (remember that the word gospel means "good news"). Jesus, with His perfectly clear jar of water, looked upon each of us with our jars of dirty water and decided to help us. He knew we could not help ourselves. Only He could help us, and He did exactly that, just like a real-life hero!

A plan was crafted to carry out Jesus' mission to clean our jars of sinful, dirty water. Here's how the plan worked:

- Jesus came to earth.
- He lived a perfect, sinless life and kept His jar of water

clean. While He was alive, His jar was clean, but our jars were still dirty.

- But then He did something amazing for us: He died, and then came alive again! With Jesus' death, His jar of beautiful, clean water was poured out. Why? So that His empty jar could be filled with our dirty water and He could fill our jar with His clean water! We could not clean our own water, but Jesus took our dirty water and replaced it with His clean water. Because He rose again, He defeated death and lets us receive His clean water and new life in Him.

Because we belong to Jesus, because He loves us, He continues to accept our dirty water and pour His beautiful, clean water into our jars.

This is the huge part of the story! Jesus took our place. He became dirty so we don't have to be anymore.

When we trust in Jesus and apologize for our sins (dirty water), He pours so much of His clean water in us that all the bad water overflows and falls out. From then on, God sees us like His Son, Jesus—clean and crystal-clear, just like Him.

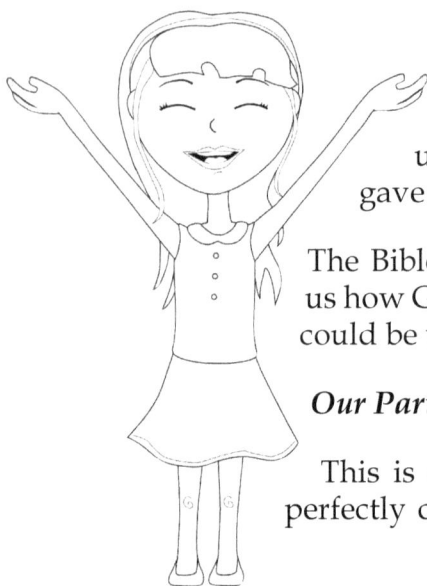

We still make mistakes, but those mistakes are forgiven because Jesus covers us. When God looks at us, all He sees is the clear water Jesus gave us, not our own filthy water.

The Bible tells us this amazing story. It tells us how God sent Jesus to make us clean so we could be with Him again.

Our Part of the Story

This is exciting because Jesus gave up His perfectly clean water so you can have it. You are a part of the story because He created you, loves you, and wants to be with you forever and ever!

He gave up everything to be with you. Jesus is the hero of the story, and when we accept Him as our Savior, we become an active part of the story He is still writing in the world. We get to team up with Him to carry out His mission on earth!

When we trust Him and decide to follow Him, He starts making us more like Himself. Remember when we talked about how cool it would be to be like your favorite superhero or character? Well, with God it is possible.

We can be like Jesus!

Now, this doesn't mean we can be exactly like Him. Even Christians mess up. No one is perfect—even if we trust Jesus with our lives.

While we should try our best to do well, doing good things isn't what's most important. What's most important is how God sees us. If we accept Jesus, God sees us just as He sees Jesus—perfect in every way. Jesus basically becomes our shield. He covers us and lets us stand with Him.

We get to be with and be like our very own superhero—Jesus.

The story of the Bible tells us all about Jesus...

- Why He came (to save us from sin)
- How He came (from heaven to earth as a human)
- When He came
- How He'll come again (to defeat Satan once and for all)
- What we can do to be like Him as we wait for Him to come back

The Bible is the best story ever. And it's one we can be a part of. This is an adventure you don't want to miss!

MaKe It YOURS!

- What is the *big* story of the Bible called?

- In your own words, what is this big story about?

- How can you be a part of His story in this world?

6

SECTION TWO: "HOW WAS IT PUT TOGETHER?"

Puzzled

Way to go! You've made it to Section Two! You now know so much about what the Bible is—how it's inerrant (without error), infallible (can't lie), inspired (a gift straight from God), living, and a great story. You're doing great!

Now we're moving into Section Two, which is all about how the Bible was put together.

Puzzled

Jimmy and Lizzy are twins. They are also best friends and enjoy doing things together—especially puzzles!

For every birthday and Christmas, they ask their parents for a puzzle. As soon as they get one, they dump all the pieces on the floor and start sorting them out. They love seeing how all the pieces fit together in color and size!

One year, something strange happened. They woke up one morning with a little red box on the floor of their living room.

"What's this?" Lizzy asked.

"I'm not sure. Let's open it!" Jimmy said.

He picked up the box and slowly removed the big yellow bow

on top. Lizzy came closer and they looked into the box as Jimmy pulled back the wrapping paper…

It was a puzzle piece!

"What are we supposed to do with a single puzzle piece?" Lizzy asked.

"I have no idea! What a weird present."

They continued talking for a few minutes, wondering who put the box there and what they were supposed to do with such a strange gift. After talking with their parents, they decided to leave it in the box and put it on their bookshelf.

Four days later, when they came home from school, Lizzy saw another little red box, but this time it was in the cookie jar.

"There's another red box, Jimmy!"

Jimmy rushed over and they opened it together. There was another puzzle piece! They both ran up to their room to see if it matched the other one. It did! Both pieces came from the same puzzle, but since they didn't have any other pieces, they decided to keep waiting for another one.

Several days later, Jimmy found another box on the bathroom counter. He and Lizzy opened it and connected it with the other two pieces they'd already found.

Over the next couple of months, they found little red boxes all over the house. They got so excited when they found one that they always immediately ran upstairs to their room to put the new piece together with the other ones.

After a long time passed, they received one final red box holding the very last piece of the puzzle. They fit in the last piece and found a little note in the box.

It was from Grandpa!

Grandpa was the one giving them the puzzle pieces! He had been sneaking over to the house and leaving the pieces so they could find them and begin the puzzle. He had all the pieces and knew they fit together, but he gave Jimmy and Lizzy only one piece at a time so they could have a special adventure putting them together.

A Puzzle of Sorts

Want to know something cool?

Though the Bible is one book, it was written over a very long period of time. There are sixty-six little books in the Bible, and God gave them to people one at a time.

Just like Jimmy and Lizzy's puzzle pieces from Grandpa, the Bible was put together piece by piece. God told people to write one book at a time, and they eventually collected all the books and put them into one big book.

Isn't that amazing? It took almost 2,000 years for the Bible to be finished and put together. That's like us living until we're 100 years old and then living again and again, 200 times in a row.

The Canon

The Bible took a very long time to write, but when it was completed, it also needed to be put together.

The sixty-six books of the Bible are split into two sections. Do you know what they are? They are the Old Testament and the New Testament. If you got that right, good job!

The Old Testament is the first part of the Bible, and the New Testament is the second part. The Old Testament has thirty-nine books, and the New Testament has twenty-seven books. Together they contain sixty-six books.

The Old Testament was written and put together a long, long time ago. The New Testament is a little newer than the Old Testament, but it is still pretty old.

All the books together have a special name (other than the Bible). It's called the *Canon*. The Canon simply refers to the books that were chosen to be in the Bible.

Because the Bible was written and collected over a very long period of time, people had to keep track of each book and keep it in a special place. Then, when all the books were finally written, people put them together so the Bible would be complete, just like a puzzle.

The Good Guys

Every book of the Bible was written by a specific person whom God chose for the job. About forty men wrote the books of the Bible.

Some writers of the books of the Bible wrote multiple books. Others wrote just one. We know who wrote most of the books, but some of the books are left anonymous.

Some writers are very popular and well-known. Others aren't known at all. Have you heard of Moses? He is a popular man in the Bible, and he wrote the first five books of the Old Testament: Genesis, Exodus, Leviticus, Numbers, and Deuteronomy.

The Apostle Paul is also a well-known writer of books in the Bible. He wrote thirteen books in the New Testament. That's a lot—over half of the New Testament!

But unlike Moses and Paul, some writers wrote only one or two books. Matthew, one of Jesus' disciples, wrote one book, the gospel of Matthew, which is the first book in the New Testament.

Amos, a prophet of the Old Testament, wrote only one book as well. And the book of Hebrews in the New Testament was left anonymous.

The writers whom God used to write the Bible were (for the most part) good men who loved and followed God.

The good guys obeyed God and wrote down the words He told them to write. But there were bad guys too.

The Bad Guys

Over time, some bad guys wrote books similar to the ones of the Bible. They told people their books were inspired by God too. But they were lying. God never inspired these people or their books.

Their lies confused people. Both the good guys and the bad guys were saying their books were from God, and God's people didn't know who was telling the truth.

It would be like two of your good friends telling you the teacher chose them as Student of the Month. That couldn't possibly be true because only one person can be named Student of the Month.

Who Wins?

So who won? The good guys or the bad guys? Let's find out.

Since so many people were writing books and claiming they were from God, the leaders and pastors of churches decided to get together. They needed to decide which books were from God and which ones weren't.

That's exactly what they did.

A couple of years after the New Testament books were completed, a group of church leaders met to decide which books should belong in the Old Testament.

This group was called the Council of Jamnia (jaw-m-nee-uh). They got together and carefully approved which thirty-nine books belonged in the Old Testament of the Bible.

A couple hundred years later, two more councils met to decide which books should be in the New Testament. These councils had very funny names! They were called the Council of Hippo (seriously!) and the Council of Carthage (car-th-ahj).

These groups determined and approved the twenty-seven books for the New Testament.

The good guys won!

How They Did It

How did the councils decide which books belonged in the Bible? Let's take a look.

1. **God told them**

   It wasn't difficult to determine which books would be included in the Bible because God already confirmed which books were the right ones. Remember the scribes we talked about before? Scribes (the people who copied and translated the first versions of Bible books) were very careful in preserving the copies of Scripture. Though some books may be anonymous to us, they were not anonymous to the people who were living back then. The scribes knew the writers of the Bible personally and knew they were writing God's words.

2. **The councils set strict standards**

   Each book of the Bible had to pass the very strict test the

councils came up with. Here are some of the standards each book was tested for[1]:

- The book must be **authoritative.** In other words, each book had to contain words claiming to be directly from God. An example would be a phrase like, "Thus says the Lord."

- The book must be **prophetic**. This means that the book had to have been written by a prophet (someone who spoke the words of God to His people), a king, a judge, a scribe, or an apostle. It must have been written by a leader who was chosen by God and recognized as a spiritual leader among the people.

- The book had to be **authentic.** If the words of the book contradicted other books of the Bible, it would not be approved. Every book had to be consistent with the rest of the Bible.

- Each book had to be **dynamic**, which means it had to show God working and confirming His truth in its words.

- The book had to be **received**. Again, when a book was completed and truly from God, God's people knew it and accepted it. Books that were not received well by the people could not have been included in the Bible.

- The book had to be **doctrinally accurate**. This simply means that it had to tell the truth about God; it couldn't have any lies in it. It had to be inerrant and infallible based on the other books of the Bible.

That's a pretty tough test, isn't it? By using these standards, the councils were able to determine which books belonged in

---

1 Litke, Sid. "Canonicity | Bible.org" http://bible.org/serisepage/canonicity.

the Bible—which ones were written by God, and which ones weren't.

The Puzzle is Complete

When the councils confirmed the books of the Bible, it was made absolutely complete. No more books could be added to it, and no one could take away from it.

Some people try to add things to the Bible and others try to take things away. That's like trying to add pieces to a completed puzzle, or take pieces away. It doesn't work! The puzzle starts looking funny when we take pieces away. And it looks odd if we add pieces that don't belong.

The Bible is a big book with lots of little books and different sections. But it is one book with one main story God is telling us—that He loves us and sent His Son so we could be with Him forever and ever.

The Bible is 100 percent complete and exactly as God wants it. It may have seemed like a sixty-six piece puzzle for a while, but in the end, God made all the pieces fit together perfectly. It is His word to us—His unified letter to people He loves.

Make It YOURS!

- How many books are in the Bible?

- Who were the "councils" and what did they do?

- How is the Bible like a puzzle? Why can't we add or take anything away from it?

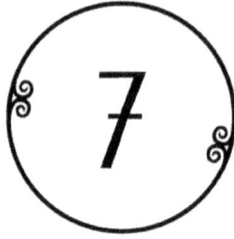

7

Say What?

We are continuing to learn all about how the Bible was put together. In the last chapter, we learned that the Bible is like a puzzle. It is made of many pieces (or books) that all fit together to form the story God wanted to tell us.

The story is wonderful. It's actually the greatest story in the whole world!

But a story doesn't do much if we don't hear about it, right? In order to enjoy a story, we have to hear it. And we can't hear it unless someone tells it to us. And we can't understand it unless someone tells it to us in a way that makes sense to us.

Milo

Milo is a little boy who was born in a terrible place in another country. His family was very poor and could not afford to provide for him the way they wanted.

One day, they sent Milo away to another city so he could be adopted by a family who could provide for him the way they wished they could have. They loved Milo and prayed that God would bring him to a wonderful family.

He soon arrived at a strange building and found many other children there too. He found out that he was going to live in the building with the other children for a long time. Slowly, he got used to to his new home and made friends with the other children.

Soon after arriving, Miss Sandra, one of the grownups who worked there, called Milo into her office. She explained to him that the children living there were waiting to be adopted.

Milo asked her, "What does 'adopted' mean?"

"It means the children here are waiting for someone to come and choose them to be a part of their family. Being adopted means getting a brand-new family — one who will love you and be able to care for your needs."

Milo liked the sound of that. He never understood why his parents sent him away, but he definitely wanted a new family who would love him and care for him. He began praying every day for a family to adopt him.

A couple of months later, he heard the best news ever. He was going to be adopted! Miss Sandra told him that a wonderful family wanted to bring him into their home and make him a part of their family.

"Do they live close by?" Milo asked excitedly.

"They live in a country called America."

"Where's that?"

"It's far away, but it's a wonderful place, and you will certainly love it!"

Milo was so excited, he barely slept that night. He was going to a land called America to live with his new mom and dad. He couldn't wait!

The day finally came for Milo to go to America. He got on the plane with his new mom and dad, who he loved very much already. But when they arrived at the airport, Milo asked his mom why people were talking funny.

"What do you mean, sweetheart?" his mom asked.

"I can't understand what they're saying!"

His mom and dad looked at each other and began explaining to Milo that people in America speak English. His mom and dad could speak Milo's language, but most people in America could speak only one. Milo would soon begin learning how to speak the funny language called English.

Milo was excited to learn how to talk like the Americans, even though he wasn't sure he'd ever be able to. They talked so fast and sounded so funny! But he was willing to learn and promised to try his very best to learn the Americans' language.

Unknown Languages

Milo experienced something that few of us every have to deal with—living in a place where people speak a different language. He learned quickly that he couldn't function very well if he didn't understand what people were saying. Fortunately, his new parents helped him a lot. They told him what the Americans were saying so he didn't have to be so confused all the time.

We can learn quite a few lessons from Milo and his journey. Did you know that the Bible was not written in English at first? Not even close!

The Bible was written in three different languages. The Old Testament was written in a language called Hebrew, and the New Testament was written in a language called Greek. A third language, Aramaic, was used in a couple of places throughout the Old and New Testaments.

Hebrew

Hebrew is a funny and strange language to us because it is very different than English. Check out a picture of it:

א בְּרֵאשִׁית בָּרָא אֱלֹהִים
אֵת הַשָּׁמַיִם וְאֵת הָאָרֶץ:

א בְּרֵאשִׁית בָּרָא אֱלֹהִים
אֵת הַשָּׁמַיִם וְאֵת הָאָרֶץ:

א בְּרֵאשִׁית בָּרָא אֱלֹהִים
אֵת הַשָּׁמַיִם וְאֵת הָאָרֶץ:

Adapted from learn-hebrew-bible.com

Doesn't that look weird?

The letters are way different than the ones in our English alphabet. The punctuation marks are different too. Hebrew doesn't use periods, commas, apostrophes, or question marks. It uses things called jots and tittles that you can see if you look at the picture very closely.

And guess what? Hebrew is read from the right side of the page to the left instead of left to right. It would take a lot of practice to get used to that!

Hebrew is one of the oldest languages in the whole world. But surprisingly, it is still spoken today. It's quite different now than it was back when the Bible was written, but some people can still read the ancient version of it.

Languages tend to change over time. For instance, there was a time when the English word "cool" meant only "cold" or "chilly." Now it means things like "awesome," "hip," and "popular."

The same thing happened in Hebrew. Over time, words changed meaning, so the Hebrew spoken today is a little different than it was back then. That means people have to work extra-hard to translate the Bible from Hebrew to English. But some great people have dedicated their lives to doing just that.

Greek

Greek is also an interesting language. Let's take a look:

μνημονεύοντες ὑμῶν τοῦ ἔργου
τῆς πίστεως καὶ τοῦ κόπου τῆς
ἀγάπης καὶ τῆς ὑπομονῆς τῆς
ἐλπίδος τοῦ κυρίου ἡμῶν
Ἰησοῦ Χριστοῦ ἔμπροσθεν τοῦ
θεοῦ καὶ πατρὸς ἡμῶν

Adapted from christilling.de

Greek looks pretty funny too, doesn't it? Greek is very different from Hebrew, but it is still not very similar to English.

For example, all the letters in biblical Greek were capitals. They didn't use lowercase letters. Also, the words were all squished together so it was hard to tell them apart. That's definitely not how we write today!

Lots of people still speak Greek today. Perhaps you know there's a country called Greece. Can you guess what language they speak? That's right—Greek!

Greek has been a popular language for a long time. In fact, dozens of languages have come from Greek as time went on. Greek was also the main language people spoke in Jesus' day. Jesus spoke Greek, Hebrew, and Aramaic (though if you think about it, He spoke every language because He knows everything!).

Like Hebrew, the Greek spoken today is very different from the way it was spoken back in biblical times. That's why scholars (very smart and educated people) have to study carefully before translating the Bible from Greek to English.

Aramaic

The third language of the Bible is Aramaic. It's different from Hebrew, Greek, and English! Take a look at an example below:

Adapted from www.everytongue.com

At this point, we expect it to look funny, don't we? Aramaic is in only twelve places in the Bible:

1. Ezra 4:8-6:18

2. Ezra 7:12-26

3. Daniel 2:4-7:28

4. Jeremiah 10:11

5. Matthew 27:46

6. Mark 5:41

7. Mark 7:34

8. Mark 14:36

9. Mark 15:34

10. Romans 8:15

11. 1 Corinthians 16:22

12. Galatians 4:6

But it is in the Bible, so it's worth a look! Aramaic, like Hebrew, is one of the world's oldest languages. It is still spoken today, but not nearly as much as Greek.

The languages of the Bible are important to know because the oldest copies of the Bible we have today are written in those languages. We wouldn't be able to translate them to English if we didn't know what languages they were in the first place. People have done a very good job of keeping up with these old languages so we can translate and understand them well today.

If the Bible was written in other languages, how did we get it in English today? And why are there so many English versions of the Bible, such as the King James Version, New Living, and the New International Version? Let's find out!

MaKe It YOURS!

- How many languages do you know?

- What three languages was the Bible written in originally?

- Why is it important to know what languages the Bible was written in at first?

8

English Please!

Remember Milo's parents? They were very sweet to help Milo when he came to America. They helped him understand what Americans were saying so he wouldn't be so confused.

Translators

Just as Milo was blessed to have parents who could translate for him, so are we blessed to have people who have translated the Bible for us.

We've already learned that scribes copied each book of the Bible carefully. Well, as the good news of Jesus spread, people from other nations started wanting to have the Bible in their language too.

Soon, churches needed translators in addition to copiers of the Bible.

The Process

Guess how many languages the Bible has been translated into? Over two thousand! That's a lot of languages!

Translating is not easy, though. One tricky part about translating is that words don't match up perfectly between languages.

Here's an example. In English, we have one word for *love*. But we use the word *love* in many different ways, don't we? We love our parents and we love pizza! We love our pets and we love playing sports. We have only one word for love, but we use it to communicate lots of different meanings.

In Greek, however, there are three different words for love. There's *phileo*, the kind of love between friends, and there's *agape*, which is deepest kind of love we can have—the kind of love that can't be broken. Then there's *eros*, the romantic love between moms and dads.

So if we were trying to translate the sentence, "My dad loves my mom," in Greek, we'd probably use either the word *agape* or *eros* because the love between moms and dads is a strong one. So if a Greek-speaking person was translating from his language into English and needed a word for the intense love between a mom and a dad, he would have to use the same word "love" that we use for loving things like ice cream!

That's one reason translating is so difficult. Words don't match other words exactly between languages.

But there's another reason it's so difficult—grammar. In English, we say "I like chicken tacos." But in Spanish the sentence would be "Me gusto los tacos de pollo," which literally means "I like the tacos of chicken."

Spanish uses different grammar rules than English. We would never say "We like the tacos of chicken." People would think we were crazy! But that's how words are arranged in Spanish.

You can now see why translating between any languages is difficult. Each language has its own vocabulary and grammatical rules that need to be followed.

But just because something is difficult doesn't mean we give up. We should be thankful that the people who translated the Bible into all those languages didn't give up.

Translators have spent years and years translating the Bible into other languages—including English. They worked hard so we could read the Bible on our own. In fact, we wouldn't have Bibles in our language at all without them!

Ways to Translate

Not only are their different types of languages, but there are also different ways to translate. The two ways are:

1. Translations

2. Paraphrases

Translations (like what we've been talking about) start with the one language and put the words into another language. Paraphrases, on the other hand, start with a book that's already been translated and reword it to make it easier to understand.

Let's explore translations first.

Translations

There are two categories of translations:

1. Translations

    . Word-for-Word

    . Thought-for-Thought

People who write word-for-word translations try to stay as close as possible to the original words. They want to be precise so they preserve the original meaning of the text.

Consider this sentence as an example:

The sun stood bright in the sky high above the mountains.

Word-for-word translations would try to translate that sentence exactly as it is written in English. They would include the main words like *sun, stood, bright, sky, high,* and *mountains* — in whatever language they were translating it to.

Their goal is to remain as close as possible to the original words they are translating.

The other type of translations is called thought-for-thought. Thought-for-thought translations are more interested in communicating the main thought or idea behind the words rather than individual words themselves.

Let's go back to our example from above:

> *The sun stood bright in the sky high above the mountains.*

A thought-for-thought translation might translate that sentence like this:

> *The sun was so high it looked higher than the mountains.*

This translation communicates the thought behind the sentence without using the exact words. That's the difference between word-for-word and thought-for-thought translations. Word-for-word translates books as closely as possible to the specific words. Thought-for-thought translates the concept or idea behind the specific words used.

Here's a real-life example from Ephesians 4:32 that will help us see the difference for ourselves.

Word-for-Word (NASB):

> *"Be kind to one another, tender-hearted, forgiving each other, just as God in Christ also has forgiven you."*

Thought-for-Thought (NIV):

> *"Be kind and compassionate to one another, forgiving each other, just as in Christ God forgave you."*

Thought-for-thoughts are a little easier to read and understand, but they also move a little farther from the original verse. Word-for-word translations, however, stay closer to the original verse in the Greek language.

Both kinds of translations are good because they translate directly from the original language. They take the Hebrew, Aramaic, and Greek manuscripts (copies) of the Bible and translate directly from them.

It's quite a complex process! A whole group of scholars gets together and begins translating the entire Bible…word by word. It takes years to do this, but they stay committed and get their job done.

Here are some examples of the different kinds of translations available in English right now:

Word-for-Word translations include:

- New American Standard Bible (NASB)
- English Standard Version (ESV)
- New King James Version (NKJV)

Thought-for-Thought translations include:

- New International Version (NIV)
- Holman Christian Standard Bible (HCS)
- Contemporary English Version (CEV)

Paraphrases

We've covered translations, now let's look at paraphrases. Paraphrases, unlike translations, start with English and simply reword it to make it easier to read.

Here's an example:

> *The dolphin leaped from the depths of the water and soared with a graceful leap over the trainer's prop.*

A paraphrase would adjust that sentence to something like:

> *The trainer held out a ball and the dolphin jumped over it to complete the trick.*

Paraphrases aren't translations because they're not converting one language into another. They simply change the words in order to make the text easier to understand.

Let's take another look at our Bible verse example, this time including paraphrases.

Word-for-Word (NASB)

> *"Be kind to one another, tender-hearted, forgiving each other, just as God in Christ also has forgiven you."*

Thought-for-Thought (NIV)

> *"Be kind and compassionate to one another, forgiving each other, just as in Christ God forgave you."*

Paraphrases (The Message)

> *"Make a clean break with all cutting, backbiting, profane talk. Be gentle with one another, sensitive. Forgive one another as quickly and thoroughly as God in Christ forgave you."*

Can you see the difference? Translations are very similar to each other, even if one chooses to focus on words and the other chooses to focus on the main thought. But paraphrases are different altogether. Their number-one priority is to make it as easy to read as possible.

Which One Should I Read?

With so many versions of the Bible, which one (or ones) should we read?

There's no magic answer. And we should never read only one version because we would miss out on the whole picture of the Bible.

Have you ever watched a movie in 3-D? Or have you seen a bookmark that changes pictures as you move it around? Looking at something in 3-D is pretty cool, isn't it? It makes plain pictures come alive and shows us more angles so we can get a better idea of what we're looking at.

Different versions make the Bible like a 3-D picture. If we read only one version, it's like looking at a flat picture. But when we read several versions, we get a more complete picture of what God is saying in the Bible.

But we can't read every version every time we read the Bible, can we? It would be pretty silly to carry a dozen Bibles to Sunday School, wouldn't it?

While reading different versions is good, there's a way we can decide which version to read more of the time.

Telephone

Have you ever played the game of telephone? One person whispers something to the person next to him, and that person tells the person next to him, and on and on. By the time the whisper gets to the last person, the sentence is rarely the same as when it started. It's funny to hear the last person say it because they frequently mess up!

The further words get from the person who spoke them first, the greater chance that the words get mixed up and changed.

Same with the Bible.

God is the original author of the Bible (Person One in the game of telephone). He told the **writers** of Scripture (Person Two in telephone) what to write, and then **copiers** (Person Three in telephone) made copies of what was written.

After that, the **word-for-word translators** (Person Four in telephone) came around, followed by the **thought-for-thought translators** (Person Five). Then came **paraphrasers** (Person Six), who took the English translations and made them a little easier to read.

As you can see, the further from God you get, the more room for error in the copies of the Bible. But this doesn't mean the versions we have today are totally unreliable like the game of telephone. It just means we have to be extra careful reading paraphrases and translations that aren't as close to the original as others.

As we said in our talk in Chapter One, God preserved His Word throughout all the years. He made sure the copiers and translators of Scripture kept His Word as He wanted it. But because humans aren't perfect, some copiers and translators make mistakes. That's why we must be careful when choosing which translations to read.

Looking at the diagram, which version of the Bible do you think would be best to read regularly? Since we can't understand the original languages of Scripture, we're left with the bottom three choices:

- Word-for-Word

- Thought-for-Thought

- Paraphrase

Which one is closest to God? If you said word-for-word, you are correct! Word-for-words are the closest versions to the original copies of Scripture. Thus, they are the most reliable English versions we have today.

Thought-for-thoughts are also good (and are much easier to read than word-for-words). Paraphrases are the furthest from the originals, so we should be careful when reading them. They can help us understand verses in the Bible, but they should never be the only versions we read because they're so far removed from the originals.

Whew! You just learned a lot about the languages and translations of the Bible. Way to go! You now have a feeling of what Milo had to learn when he began studying another language.

Thankfully, we don't have to learn the ancient languages of the Bible in order to read it. Translators have done an amazing job translating them for us. But it's definitely important to remember that the English versions we have today are not the original versions of Scripture. The Bible is the most important book in the world, and we must do our best to learn as much about it (and its author, God) as possible.

That's what we're going to talk about next. Ready to move on to Section Three? Let's do it!

MaKe It YOURS!

- How many languages has the Bible been translated into?

- Why is translating the Bible difficult?

- What are the two *ways* to translate?

- What version of the Bible is your favorite?

9

SECTION THREE "YOUR Faith"

use the ROPe!

Jeremy knows a lot about water skiing. His parents have been professional skiers since they were little kids, and all their friends ski too.

Their house is filled with his parents' trophies and medals from skiing competitions, and their rooms are cluttered with action posters of famous skiers doing tricks on the water.

Jeremy could tell you anything you want to know about the sport. He knows everything about the best boats, the best skis, and the best ropes to get maximum height on all the tricks.

He also knows the best time of day to go, when the water is too rough to ski, and how it's safest to have at least two people on the boat when one person is skiing.

Jeremy could be considered an expert (a skilled, smart person) on the sport of skiing, but he'd never skied until last Saturday.

For some reason, Jeremy was never interested in skiing. Even though his parents love skiing, he never tried it. He preferred sports like basketball and baseball, and he played on a couple of teams throughout the year.

But last Saturday, he decided to go skiing for the first time.

He was in for the surprise of his life.

Jeremy quickly realized that knowing about something doesn't mean you know it experientially (personally). He knew a lot about skiing, but doing it was completely different!

Skiing was difficult! He mistakenly thought that because he knew so much about skiing, it would be easy for him. His parents were professionals, after all. Surely he had their talent!

But when he tried it, he learned that his parent's skill didn't make him a good skier. He'd have to learn and practice on his own if he wanted to become good at it.

Knowing Isn't Enough

We just learned a lot about the Bible, didn't we? We learned what it is, how it was put together, who wrote it, what languages it was written in, and more. You're doing great!

Learning is awesome, especially when it's about the Bible—the best book in the world!

But as we just learned from Jeremy's story, knowing facts about the Bible doesn't mean you know it on a personal level. Jeremy knew a lot about skiing, but he didn't put any of his knowledge into practice until he actually tried to ski.

God wrote the Bible to tell us about Himself and how we are a part of His story through Jesus. If we only learn facts about the Bible and never let it help us grow in our relationships with God, then all our learning doesn't accomplish much.

Like Jeremy, we need do more than just learn facts. We need to know and be in a relationship with the Bible's Author, God.

Is it Alive for You?

Remember how we talked about the Bible being alive? The Holy Spirit works with the Bible and makes it come alive in our hearts and minds. He uses it to teach us things, help us make good decisions, and instruct us in ways to help others when they need it.

We must remember that the Holy Spirit helps the Bible come alive only to Christians—those who have accepted Jesus Christ as their Savior. When we become Christians, Jesus pours His clean water into our jars of dirty water and makes us clean, like He is.

Being a Christian is a personal decision each of us has to make. Our parents might be wonderful Christians who take us to church every week. But just because your parents are Christians doesn't mean you are one.

Just like Jeremy, we must realize that while our parents can help us understand faith, we have to do something about it ourselves in order to make it our own. We have to act on the information they give us; otherwise, it just stays in our brains and isn't good for much of anything!

Becoming a Christian is similar to skiing—we must do it for ourselves. Just as we must make a decision to get off the boat and into the water when we ski, we must decide to accept Jesus as our Savior and begin a new life in Him.

The Bible is like the ski rope of our faith. Once we decide to follow Jesus, the Bible helps us stay connected to God. Unlike the ski rope, however, the Bible never lets go of us! Even if we mess up, it's always there for us. (And so is God.) The Bible helps us get back on track and correct our mistakes. It's way better than a ski rope, for sure!

But people who don't know Jesus can't use the Bible correctly. To them, the Bible is like a stiff rope that doesn't move. People can know about it, but it doesn't help them get up on the skis of life until they choose to believe in it.

If we haven't made a decision to become a son or daughter of

God, then everything we've learned about the Bible is good, but it's not going to help us live a life of faith. Just like Jeremy, we will have lots of information about the Bible, but it will not be real to us until we do something about it.

Jeremy had to try skiing before everything he knew about it made sense. Same with the Bible. We need to accept Jesus and commit our lives to Him before the Bible will come alive and make sense to us.

Have You Made a Decision?

Have you made a decision about Jesus? Do you believe that He is God—that He came to earth to die for us so our sins could be washed away? Have you talked to Him about it in prayer, asking Him to forgive you for your sins and to rescue you…to be your real-life hero?

If you have, awesome! Keep going strong and using the Bible to keep you close to God's heart.

If you haven't, Jesus wants nothing more than to be your real-life hero. If you haven't decided to follow Him yet, you can—right this minute—if you want!

Just take a minute or two, either by yourself or with a parent, pastor, or Sunday School teacher, and pray a prayer that sounds something like this,

> Dear God,
>
> Thank you for loving me so much! I am not perfect at all. I've messed up a lot and have sinned many times. Even when I try to be good, I don't always succeed. Please forgive me for my sins. On my own, I'm not good enough to be with You in heaven; yet You love me so much You sent Your Son to rescue me!

Today I choose to believe in and follow You. I want to become Your son (or daughter) in Jesus!

I believe Jesus came to this earth and lived a perfect life for me. I believe He died on the cross so I could be made clean like You. I believe He rose again on the third day to defeat sin and to make a way for me to be with You forever in heaven!

Please come live in my heart and my life, Jesus. I want to live for You from now on. I want to get out of the boat and start living life with You. I trust You and want to spend the rest of my life following You and becoming more like Jesus every day! Thank You for saving me!

In Jesus' Name,

Amen

If you just prayed that prayer and meant it, YAY!!!! God prepared you for this moment and welcomes you into His family as His child. The angels are throwing a party in heaven right this very minute! They are celebrating a brand new child of God—YOU!

Here's what you do now. First, find an adult who is a Christian (one of your parents, someone at your church or school) and tell them that you decided to follow Jesus. They will be excited for you and will help you in your new journey of faith.

Second, you'll probably want to get baptized one day soon, so you can show people that you're in God's family now!

Third, you are now a new person in Jesus. You are God's son or daughter, which means your life is going to change. Jesus is more than your best friend; He's your King. You now live for Him — seeking to serve Him and love Him in everything you say, think and do.

You get the chance to make God smile with how you live! Every time you read the Bible and talk to Jesus in prayer, you make God smile. Every time you are nice to someone, sing songs to God, and ask Him to make you more like Jesus, it brings a smile to His face. You now belong to the King of the universe and get to become more like Him every day if you put Him first.

Welcome to God's family! You are now a part of the greatest family in the whole, wide world! You just inherited thousands of brothers and sisters who love you — including me (Mindi Jo Furby)! Every Christian is now your brother or sister in Jesus. Isn't that exciting? You are loved more than you could ever know, and you have lots of people cheering for you!

Get ready for the adventure of a lifetime. And congratulations on getting out of the boat!

Owning Your Faith

What you're doing right now — learning, believing, and growing in your faith — is important. It's especially important for you to realize it's a journey you should take seriously.

Accepting Jesus in your heart is awesome, but it's only the first step. It's kind of like getting up on your skis for the first time. You don't get up and immediately let go on purpose…that would be silly!

Instead, you hold onto the rope (the Bible) and continue letting it lead you in your life. There will be times you trip and mess up, but now that you're a Christian, you can always get back up and keep going.

That's what the Christian life and faith are all about — moving forward toward Jesus. We get to spend the rest of eternity with Him, and now we can use the rest of our lives on this earth to fall more in love with Him.

We'll also start becoming like Jesus. Through the Bible and the Holy Spirit, God will begin changing us for the better. He'll make us more friendly, more compassionate, wiser, stronger (in faith), and a better person all around.

How amazing is that? That's what happens when we not only learn about the Bible, but we use it to move us closer to God. It's not good enough to know about ski ropes. We need to use them in order to have a great time and go on the grand adventure of a lifetime!

Remember that as we move into our last section—how to read the Bible and apply it to our lives.

Make It YOURS!

- Is knowing *about* God and the Bible enough to have faith? Why or why not?

- Is your parents' faith enough to cover you? Why or why not?

- Have you made a personal decision to follow Jesus? If not, what's stopping you?

10

SECTION FOUR "HOW to Read It"

HERMEN...What?!

Megan was nervous as she walked up the steps to her new classroom. Her family had just moved to the area from another state, and this was her first day at her new school.

Some kids at her other school teased her about being a nerd. She was smart and wore glasses, and she always got straight As on her report card. But for some reason, she never fit in with other kids. She always got nervous and shy when anyone talked to her.

Not this time, though. At this school, Megan was determined to make friends. So when she opened the door and watched as all the kids turned to look at her, she smiled and tried to look friendly.

The teacher, Mr. White, introduced Megan to the class and showed her where she would sit. Then he told her what they were learning about today — ciphers (secret codes).

Megan was fascinated with the lesson. She learned that during historical wars, each side used ciphers to hide their messages to each other from the enemy.

Mr. White even gave the class an example of a secret code. It was called the Reverse Alphabet Cipher, and it looked like this:

A	B	C	D	E	F	G	H	I	J	K	L	M
Z	Y	X	W	V	U	T	S	R	Q	P	O	N

N	O	P	Q	R	S	T	U	V	W	X	Y	Z
M	L	K	J	I	H	G	F	E	D	C	B	A

Every cipher needs a key, which is what the picture above is for the Reverse Alphabet Cipher. Mr. White explained that people who use the code write out the blue letters, but they secretly mean the red letters. Here's an example:

DLFOW	BLF	ORPV	Z	XLLPRV?
WOULD	YOU	LIKE	A	COOKIE?

Megan was excited to learn about these secret codes. She started practicing and coming up with her own ciphers, and the kids in her class thought the ciphers were cool!

Soon Megan was making lots of friends, and they all wrote secret messages to each other. They had so much fun that it became the class's hobby.

Secret Code for the Bible?

Megan learned that secret codes are fascinating and make notes fun to read because there's a secret meaning behind them. But she also learned that without the proper cipher key, no one can understand the notes.

Want to learn another fun fact? The Bible has its very own cipher key! It's not as intense (hard) as secret codes that use different letters or symbols, but if we ignore or don't use the key, there's a good chance we won't understand what the Bible is saying.

The cipher key is called hermeneutics (pronounced "her – men – new – ticks"). That's an awfully big word. But it's also fun and something not many people know about!

Hermeneutics

Hermeneutics simply means "how to read, interpret, and apply the Bible correctly to our lives." As we've discovered, the Bible isn't a normal book. It's special because it's God's Word to us. So we need to learn to read, interpret, and apply it in the way He means us to.

The Bible has four "rules" of hermeneutics that will help us understand it (break its "code").

1. **It Means What It Says** (The Literal, Grammatical and Historical Method)

2. **Context** (We must understand the context or background of what we're reading)

3. **God is Smarter than We Are...and so is His Word!** (Scripture is our authority; we are not higher than it)

4. **Get the Big Picture** (Scripture interprets Scripture)

We're going to take the next couple of chapters to go through each of these rules. They are keys to help us understand what the Bible is saying. Let's get started!

Make It YOURS!

- What is the cipher key for the Bible called?

- What are the four "rules" that help us "decode" the Bible?

11

It Means What It Says

"That's not what I said!" Bobby yelled.

"Dude, relax. You'll get another chance next year," Jake said.

His cheeks hot with anger, Bobby walked away. He couldn't stand Jake. Whenever Bobby said anything, Jake always twisted his words and used them against him. Jake often embarrassed him in front of all their friends, and Bobby was tired of it.

This time Jake had gone too far.

Bobby dreamed about being in the city's youth orchestra since he was little. He practiced the saxophone every day, waiting to get old enough to try out. He knew he played well and was excited to show Mr. Smith, the conductor, his skills.

Like everyone else in Bobby's life, Jake knew how much he wanted to be in the orchestra. Bobby talked about it constantly. "I would give anything to be on the orchestra," he often said. "My parents are so great, they worked extra jobs to pay for my private sax lessons."

One day, Jake went to dinner with his parents, who were good friends with Mr. Smith, the orchestra conductor. When they got to the restaurant, Mr. Smith saw them and invited them to eat with him.

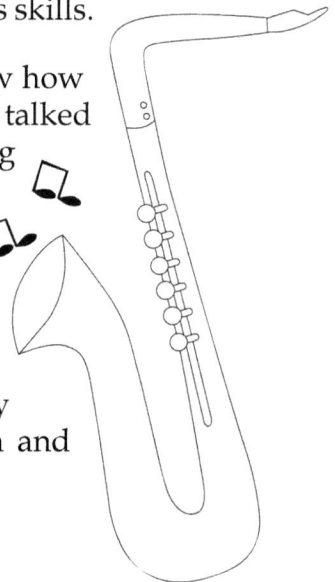

83

Jake was excited because he knew his friend Bobby was trying to impress Mr. Smith. He could talk to Mr. Smith about how great Bobby was…or maybe he could play a little practical joke instead.

After the waiter brought their food, Jake told Mr. Smith he had a friend who was going to try out for the orchestra.

"What's his name?" Mr. Smith said.

"Bobby, and he's a good saxophone player."

"Wow, that's great. We need a good saxophone player this year."

"He's good," Jake said, "but he's not the nicest guy in the world."

"What do you mean?"

"He's obsessed with being on the orchestra and will do whatever it takes to be in it. He wants to make it so badly he told his parents they had to pay for private lessons so he'd be good enough. But they don't have much money, so he whined and made them feel guilty, so they eventually decided to do it. Like I said, Bobby's not very nice."

"That's too bad," Mr. Smith said. "I'll have to remember that."

A couple of weeks later, Bobby stood on the stage, having just completed his saxophone audition. Though he was nervous, he thought his performance went well. He was excited to hear what Mr. Smith would say.

When everyone had finished auditioning, Mr. Smith read the names of those who had made the orchestra.

Bobby's name was not called.

Heartbroken, Bobby walked up to Mr. Smith. Maybe he could ask him why he didn't make it and see if there was anything he could work on so he could do better next year.

Mr. Smith put a hand on Bobby's shoulder and told them he did well in his audition.

"Then why didn't I make it?"

"Well, to be honest, I heard some things about you that concerned me. Namely, that you aren't a very nice person. Our orchestra is a close group, and we have no room for people who aren't pleasant to be around. Maybe if you work on your attitude, there will be room for you next year."

"What? Who told you that?"

"I'm not comfortable sharing that with you, but I will say that it's someone who knows you pretty well."

Bobby was crushed. Who could have told him such awful things? Who would ruin his chance to get in the orchestra?

A couple of days later, Bobby found out when he told Jake the story of what Mr. Smith said.

Jake snickered. "Aw, I'm sorry, Bobby. I may have played a little joke on you. Mr. Smith didn't understand it, I guess."

And he told Bobby what he'd said.

"That's not what I said!" Bobby yelled.

"Dude, relax. You'll get another chance next year."

That day, Bobby learned the importance of keeping people's words straight. Jake had made him feel awful, and he promised never to do that to anyone.

It Means What It Says

One of the "cipher keys" of hermeneutics is remembering that the Bible means what it says. If God tells us to honor, respect, and obey our parents, it means that we should do just that.

Some people, like Jake, like to take the words of the Bible and twist them to mean things it clearly doesn't say. Let's look at Galatians 3:28 as an example,

There is neither Jew nor Greek, there is neither slave nor free man, there is neither male nor female; for you are all one in Christ Jesus.

In this verse, God tells us we are all equal in status and worth in Jesus. No one is more important than anyone else, and God doesn't love some people more than others.

But some people make this verse say something that it doesn't. They think it means there is no difference between races (white, black, Asian, Hispanic, etc.) or boys and girls. That's just silly. Of course there are differences! Boys are not exactly the same as girls, and people look different from each other. Some have black hair, others have blonde. Some have dark skin; others have light. How boring would it be if we were all the same?

But some people refuse to use our Cipher Key #1 when reading the Bible: **The Bible Means What it Says.**

We should not twist the words of the Bible as Jake did with Bobby's words. We must respect what God says in His Word and remember that it means what it says.

It's Literal

Do you know what the word "literal" means? It means "actual, true…a matter of fact, accurate."[2] Basically, if something is literal, it's not exaggerated (made out to be a bigger deal than it is).

The following statement is literal:

The building is 500 feet high.

The building is actually 500 feet tall. It reaches 500 feet into the air.

_____
2 http://dictionary.reference.com/browse/literal

86

It would not be literal to change the sentence to this:

The building is a monster that looms over everything else around it.

This second statement communicates that the building is high, but it is not literal because the building is not actually a monster. This is called *figurative language*. It makes a point, but it's not literal. It exaggerates the facts (which are that the building is actually 500 feet tall).

Since the Bible means what it says, we can read it literally. When it tells us David killed Goliath with a stone and sling, it means that David really did kill Goliath with a stone and sling. He didn't kill him with a boulder, nor was "stone" a secret word for a bow and arrow. David killed Goliath with a stone and sling.

The Bible should always be read literally, unless the grammatical context (the grammar of the words being used) demands otherwise.

It's Grammatical

The only exception to the "rule" of reading the Bible literally is when God uses figurative language (mentioned above) to make a point.

The Bible, in addition to being literal, also follows normal rules of grammar. As you know from school, grammar is the study of a particular language — its sentences, structure, and special features. Nouns and verbs are a part of grammar. So are things like similes (comparisons using "like" or "as") and metaphors (comparisons without using the words "like" or "as").

This is important to understand because sometimes the grammar of a Bible verse makes it impossible to read literally.

Here's an example for you:

First Peter 5:8 says,

> *"Be of sober spirit, be on alert. Your adversary, the devil, prowls around like a roaring lion, seeking someone to devour."*

In this verse, the Apostle Peter warns the church to be on guard against the devil. He could have said something like this,

> *"Watch out because the devil is out to get you."*

But he chose to say it a different way. He wanted to get the readers' attention, so he decided to use a simile (a comparison using "like" or "as"). Instead of simply saying the devil is out to get them, Peter compared the devil to a big lion that roars and walks around, looking for someone to attack.

This simile gets our attention, doesn't it? Which is scarier — a bad guy to watch out for or a roaring lion that's prowling around, waiting to attack you?

The giant, mean lion is much scarier!

That's why Peter used a figure of speech in this instance. The devil is real, but he is not a lion. He *is* a bad guy and acts *like* a lion — seeking out people to destroy.

Peter uses a figure of speech to communicate truth. This leads us to our next important point:

> *Always take the Bible seriously, even when we can't always take it literally.*

Again, there will be times when we discover figures of speech in the Bible and we can't take it literally. But we can always take the verses and passages seriously.

We can count on David's sling and stone being just as serious as Peter's warning about the devil being like a lion. Both are serious, despite one being literal and the other using figurative language.

It doesn't matter if God uses a figure of speech or a declarative statement to tell us something. We can always take Him seriously and learn the truth He's communicating through His Word.

It's Historical

We've learned two parts of the first "hermeneutics cipher" — literal and grammatical. Now let's discover the third part: the Bible is historical.

What does historical mean? Does it mean it's old? Or that it talks about history?

Yes and yes! But it also means much more.

Saying the Bible is historical means...

1) It tells us history accurately.

> In some ways, the Bible is like our history books in school. It tells us stories of what has taken place in history. But unlike our history books, the Bible is perfect. It doesn't make any mistakes. Our history books sometimes get things wrong, but the Bible doesn't. Remember the terms for that? That's right! Inerrancy and infallibility!

2) It gives us God's perspective.

> The history books we use in school are written by men and women who tell us things they think are important for us to know. They tell us about wars, politics, discoveries, and inventions — all kinds of things they think we should know. These things are good to know about, but they don't necessarily tell us anything about God or faith in Jesus.

But the Bible does. It doesn't just tell us interesting facts of what happened a long time ago. Through the Bible, God tells us what He thinks is important for us to know. No normal history books can do that.

God uses the Bible to give us insight into what He thinks, feels, and wants our lives to be like.

3) It's true.

The characters and stories within the pages of the Bible are 100 percent true. When we read about Jonah being swallowed by a big fish, we can be sure there was a real man named Jonah, and he was swallowed by a big fish!

Every story in the Bible is true and teaches us about God and how we can become more like Jesus.

4) It was written by specific people, to specific people, at a specific time, and for a specific purpose.

Remember when we talked about how the Bible was put together? Each book of the Bible was written by a real person as they were inspired by God. The gospel of Matthew (the first book in the New Testament) was written by the Apostle Matthew.

The authors also wrote to specific people — either a person or a group of people. Matthew wrote his gospel letter primarily to a group of people — the Jewish people.

Each book was also written at a specific time in history, just like you write your homework assignments on specific dates so you can turn them in on time.

Lastly, each book was also written for a specific purpose. Turning our attention back to Matthew, we learn that he wrote his gospel letter to convince the Jews that Jesus is their Messiah (Savior, Lord, King). That was his entire purpose of writing the book of Matthew.

As we can see, the Bible is historical. It tells us what happened in the past and shows us what God thinks is important.

As we read the Bible, we need to remember that it is historical. The books we read in it are written by and for specific people. God definitely teaches us His truth through it, but each of these books was written specifically for someone else, so we need to be careful how we read and apply them to our lives. We don't want to assume God is speaking directly to us in every verse… but this is something we'll learn about in the next chapter.

Congrats! You've learned the first three parts of the Bible cipher that helps us read and understand it correctly. First, the Bible is literal and can always be taken seriously, even if it uses figurative language. Second, it's grammatical, meaning it uses figures of speech (metaphors, similes, hyperboles, etc.) to teach us truth in exciting ways. And finally, it is historical—written by real people who were addressing (writing to) people for a particular purpose.

Now let's turn our attention to the next "code" that will help us understand the Bible!

Make It YOURS!

- Does the Bible mean what it says?

- What does "literal" mean?

- Are there any exceptions to reading the Bible literally?

- How is the Bible historical?

12

The W's: Who, What, When, Where, and Why

Jenna loves movies. Her room is littered with posters of her favorite movie stars, and she dreams of being a famous actress one day.

One of her family's favorite weekend activities is going to see a movie and then talking about it over dinner afterward. They love talking about the characters, the story, if it was good or bad, and what they think could have made it even better.

On a summer Saturday afternoon, Jenna found herself getting impatient. Dad was out of town on a business trip, and her mom was supposed to take her to the movie theater at 2 p.m. But Mom had to run to the grocery store, so she planned to pick Jenna up at 1:45 so they could make the movie on time.

Well, the clock read 1:55, and Jenna's heart was beating fast. She wanted her mom to get home now so they could make it to the movie! Sure enough, Mom made it home and they left for the theater.

Unfortunately, they were late. Really late.

They arrived at the theater at 2:30, after getting stuck in a traffic jam. Jenna was so disappointed! They decided to watch the movie anyway and slowly made their way through the crowds into the dark theater.

As they walked in, they saw two characters on the screen. They were in deep conversation, saying things that didn't make sense to Jenna and her mom at all. The characters were talking about someone named Tom, who they were apparently angry with. Jenna had no idea who Tom was and found herself confused. She was upset that she had no idea what was going on.

She and her mom waited a few minutes and then began packing up to leave the movie.

"That was strange," Jenna said to her mom.

"Yes, it was. I have no idea what was going on. Who was Tom? I didn't get it at all."

"I guess we don't have much to talk about over dinner tonight," Jenna sighed.

"No, I suppose not. But, hey, let's go get ice cream and not let it ruin our day."

Jenna and her mom left and headed for the local ice cream shop.

The W's

Jenna and her mom realized an important lesson that day—one that we need to know in order to understand (and "decode") the Bible correctly.

Everything has CONTEXT and we must pay attention to it!

Do you know what context is? Perhaps you've learned about it in school or your mom or dad has explained it to you.

The dictionary definition is:

The set of circumstances or events in which a particular event occurs; the language surrounding a particular use of a word.[3]

---

3 www.wordsmith.net

Basically, context is the story surrounding everything in our lives. It can also be referred to as the W's—the Who, What, When, Where, and Why of something that's happening.

Every event, song, sport, activity, and situation in our lives has a context. Jenna and her mom learned that even movie scenes have context. We can't walk into the middle of a movie and expect to know what's going on because we don't know the W's of the scene. We don't know who is talking, what is going on, when it is taking place, where they are, or why they are discussing what they're discussing.

The same can be said of our lives. Here are some examples:

- Each of our classes in school has a context

  o Who: teachers/students

  o What: what you're learning

  o When: what time of day

  o Where: what school/classroom

  o Why: why you're there

- Our friendships have a context

  o Who: the names of our friends

  o What: what kind of friendship you have

  o When: what ages you are, how long you've been friends

  o Where: where your friendship usually occurs— school, sports, etc.

  o Why: why you're friends (similar personalities, same interests, etc.)

- Our activities have contexts

  - Who: who you perform the activities with

  - What: what kind of activity it is/ the rules associated with it

  - When: the time you do the activity, practices and games, etc.

  - Where: where the activity takes place

  - Why: why you enjoy it or why your parents are making you do it

As you can see, our lives are filled with different contexts, and each one has different W's. We usually know the W's automatically. We don't often think about the W's or context of our activities or parts of our lives. But when two activities cross paths, context suddenly becomes important.

Let's pretend you are a tennis player and have a big tournament coming up. You practice and practice until you finally feel ready to compete.

You show up at the tournament to discover someone had given you the wrong address. Instead of a tennis tournament, you stumble upon a golf tournament! You have no idea how to play golf, and you certainly can't join the tournament because you don't know the context (the W's) of the game.

You'd probably get right back in the car, huh? Or maybe watch for a while to try to figure out what golf is all about.

When we learn something new (like a sport or hobby), we first try to understand its context. If we don't understand who's playing, what they are doing, when or where they are doing it, or why they are doing it, we don't have much hope for being able to participate.

Everything in life has a context, and the Bible does too.

Every book, chapter, passage, and verse of the Bible has its very own context. Is it possible to flip open a new book to a random page, start reading it, and then understand exactly what's going on? Of course not! We have to start in the beginning to have a good understanding of the context of what we're reading.

The same is true with the Bible. In order to understand it well (and break its "code"), we must answer the W questions that give it context. Let's dive into an example, shall we?

Philippians 4:13 is one of the most famous verses in the Bible. It says,

> *"I can do all things through Him (Jesus) who strengthens me."*

Famous athletes quote this verse when they win a sporting event. Actors and actresses say it sometimes, and people who accomplish something important in life say this when they want to include Jesus in their victories.

While this seems pretty straightforward at first glance, if we don't examine the context, we'll miss out on a lot of its meaning.

The "W's" of Context for Philippians 4:13

WHO

The Apostle Paul wrote this verse to the church of Philippi—a church located in the region (city/town) called Philippi. Paul is the first *Who*—being the man whom the verse came from. The second *Who* is the Philippian church, being the people who were receiving the letter.

WHAT

What is Paul trying to tell the Philippian church? If we read the whole letter (the book of Philippians), we learn that Paul is encouraging the church to remain close together and to be joyful in Jesus, no matter what they go through.

By reading the verses closest to our verse (Philippians 4:13), we realize that Paul is talking about how he has endured (gone through) difficult times in his life and faith. He went several times without meals, as well as without any money at all. We learn from other passages that he was beaten, stoned (people threw rocks at him, trying to kill him), was shipwrecked, and many more horrible things because of his faith.

His point in this verse is that he has learned to be content in any and every circumstance he goes through. Why? Because Jesus lives in and with him! Paul can endure anything in life because he knows his strength comes from Jesus, not his own efforts.

That's also the *What* of this verse. Paul is telling the Philippians to be like him—content no matter what they are going through in life because Jesus gives them strength to get through everything.

This is important because we now understand that this verse applies to much more than just winning athletic events and getting good grades on tests. Jesus gives us the strength to get through awful circumstances as well as good ones. We need to rely on Him during hard times as well as when things are great. All our strength comes straight from Him if we are Christians.

WHEN

We should always try to find out *When* the verse was written so we can better understand what was going on in history at the time.

The book of Philippians was written in AD 63 or 64. That

is a really long time ago! Around 2,000 years ago, to be more specific.

There are two categories of time—B.C. (which stands

B.C.	A.D.
(Before Christ)	(Anno Domini)

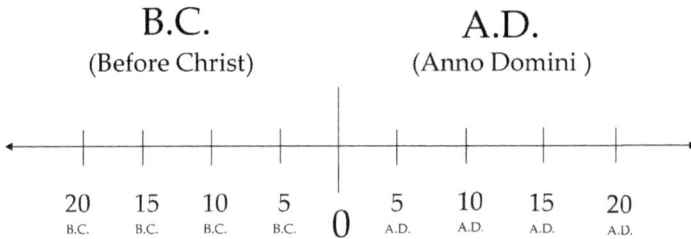

for "before Christ,") and A.D. (which stands for Anno Domini, meaning "the year of our Lord"). Here's what it looks like:

Jesus was born around the year 0. His birth changed how the world kept track of time! Isn't that amazing?

So, Paul wrote the letter of Philippians in the year 63/64 A.D., which was very close to the time when Jesus was alive. Jesus died around 33 A.D., which means Paul wrote Philippians about thirty years later.

WHERE

Where was Paul and *Where* were the Philippians when he wrote our verse, Philippians 4:13?

Paul wrote the book of Philippians when he was in prison in Rome. Paul was in prison because he loved Jesus and other people didn't want him to. Isn't that crazy? The Roman government made Paul a prisoner because of his faith! Yet instead of obeying the Romans, he continued strong in his faith and even wrote letters to churches while he was in prison.

The region of Philippi was located in northeastern Greece a long time ago. The church of Philippi met in houses, and Paul's letter was passed around to the church groups that met in that area.

WHY

Why did Paul write our verse and the letter of Philippians in general? We mentioned this in the *WHAT* section, but Paul wanted to encourage the church of Philippi. He wanted to remind them to stay close with one another because that's how God intended us to be. He also wanted them to remain joyful and content in their faith, just as he was.

Can you now see how understanding the context helps us understand the verse so much better? Before, Philippians 4:13 seemed basic and simple. But now, after learning about its context, we see it in a whole new way. A black and white picture of the verse has now bloomed into brilliant and vibrant color!

That's why context is such an important tool to help us "decode" the meaning of the Bible. If we never looked into the context of the verses we read, then we would miss out on a whole bunch of what God is trying to tell us!

Just as Jenna and her mom missed out on the whole point of the movie because they didn't understand the context of the scene, we can miss out on the point of the Bible and the verses within it if we don't pay attention.

A Great Tool

How are we supposed to find out all that great information and context of the Bible? One great tool is a study Bible. Study Bibles write out much of the context before each book of the Bible, so we can read that to better understand what we're reading in Scripture.

Study Bibles also have lots of maps we can look at to see where different stories and books are happening, and they have explanations at the bottom of each page that help us better understand the verses we read.

A wonderful study Bible is the *ESV Grow!* Bible, which contains lots of resources to help you read and understand the context of the Bible. If you do not have a study Bible, try asking your parents for one…maybe for your birthday or Christmas. If not, see if your church has a study Bible available for you to use (many churches do!).

As we've seen, context is important and helps us understand what God is saying in His Word. From now on, when you read the Bible, read the verses around whatever verse you're reading, and if you can, read the notes in a study Bible to help you even more!

Make It YOURS!

- In your own words, explain what *context* means.

- Does everything in life have a context? Even the Bible?

- How does context help us understand what we read in the Bible?

13

God is Smarter than We Are...and So is His Word!

Juan has a little sister named Maria, who just turned two years old. He cares for her and loves to play with her, even though she doesn't understand how to play very much yet.

He sits on the floor with her and rolls a ball back and forth, and he enjoys watching her laugh as the ball rolls away. He also plays pick-a-boo with her, which makes her cheeks turn pink because she laughs so much.

Juan will do whatever he can to make Maria smile because he loves her.

One day, Juan was chasing Maria around the room when she walked over to the wall and sat down. Giggling, she looked at Juan, a huge smile on her face. Then she glanced at the wall and saw an electrical outlet plug. She began to reach for it when Juan yelled, "No!" as loud as he could.

He knew that sticking her fingers in the plug would cause Maria to get electrocuted (shocked), and she could die from it. Maria stopped immediately, but a couple minutes later she tried to touch it again.

"Maria, no!" Juan yelled again. "You can't touch that or you'll get hurt!"

Because he was older and smarter, Juan knew the outlet would hurt Maria. Maria thought she could touch the outlet and be fine. She wouldn't listen to Juan at first because she thought she knew better than he did. But she was young and immature, and her actions almost caused her to get hurt.

Maria finally listened to him, but only after Juan had warned her several times.

We're like Maria

When it comes to understanding God and His Word, we are more like Maria than Juan. God is a lot smarter than we are (He knows everything, after all), and He wants what is best for us. His Word contains much more wisdom than we could ever hope to have, so it's wise for us to read it and obey what He says.

Just as Juan knew better than Maria about the outlet, God knows much better than we do about how to live a good life that pleases Him. God doesn't talk out loud to us as Juan talked to Maria, but He does talk to us through His Word. And we had better pay attention; otherwise, we could get hurt and make lots of mistakes.

The Ultimate Authority

Do you know what the word "authority" means? It is the person who is in charge. Your mom and dad have authority over you. They can tell you what to do because they know what's best for you. They are older and wiser than you, which is why they make most of the decisions around the house and with life in general.

Teachers, coaches, and other parents have authority over you too. For the most part, they all have more wisdom than you do, and they know how life works better than you do (even though it may not seem like it sometimes). They can help you make good decisions and avoid getting hurt.

Authority is not a bad thing. It's a very good thing when it's done right. Juan was an authority figure over Maria, and if he hadn't used his authority to stop her, she would've gotten hurt.

God is the best authority figure alive. He loves us more than we can understand and wrote the Bible so we could always have something to go to when we have a question or want to become smarter and wiser.

Since God is in authority over us, His Word is too! God's words in the Bible stand in authority over us. That means we are supposed to listen to and obey every word because we can trust that God loves us and wants what's best for us.

We are not the boss of God or the Bible. We cannot pick and choose what we want to read or what to listen to or what to obey. We must submit (willingly listen to and obey) everything the Bible says because God wrote it and He is our Heavenly Daddy.

The Problem

When we don't listen to what God says in the Bible, we get hurt. We may not get hurt physically (with our bodies) like Maria almost did, but we do get hurt spiritually (with our faith in God), emotionally (how we feel), and mentally (how we think).

The Bible teaches us how to act—what to do and what not to do. But God also shows us how to think, feel, and mature (grow up) in our relationships with Jesus.

If we don't listen to what God says in the Bible, we cannot benefit from His promises. For instance, in Romans 8:28, God promises to work out everything in our lives for our good. That means that every single event, relationship, and circumstance in our lives happens for a reason, and ultimately for our good in the end.

God can even use a bad test score for our good! If we get a bad grade, He can use it to teach us the value of studying harder, getting help, and maybe how to be more responsible. God promises to work things out for good if we love and trust Him.

But if we don't listen to Him and this promise, we'll miss out on the good He wants to teach us. If we get a bad grade and refuse to believe His promise, we won't learn the lesson He is trying to teach us. We probably won't become wiser through it as He wants us to.

When we think we know better than God and ignore Him (like Maria thought she knew better than Juan), we are the ones who are wrong and can miss out on what He plans for us.

God is much smarter than we are. He created us! He knows us better than we could ever know ourselves. He's also perfect, which means He doesn't make any mistakes.

So if we listen to Him and what He says in His Word, we will be far better off than we are when we do things our way. Maria almost got badly injured when she tried to do what she wanted to do. But when she listened to Juan, she was safe and made the right decision, even if she didn't understand it all at the time.

David Thought He Knew Better than God

One man in the Bible thought he was smarter than God. Of course, he would never say that out loud, but his actions proved that he didn't think highly of God or His Word.

This man's name was David. David loved God a lot and tried his best to do everything God told him to do. But that all changed one day.

David saw a pretty girl and wanted to be her husband. There was one problem though—she was already married to someone else! David knew that God would want him to leave her alone, but David didn't listen. He thought he knew better than God, so he took her and eventually had her husband killed!

We've all messed up, but not many people have had someone killed before!

David made a very bad decision, which he paid for in lots of ways. But his first problem was that he didn't listen to God. He put himself in authority over God, and it messed everything up.

Bad things happen when we don't listen to God through the Bible. Sure, we may have fun for a minute as David did when he got what he thought he wanted. But that fun doesn't last long, and when it's over, we find ourselves crushed and wishing we could go back and listen to our ultimate authority—God.

What if?

What if Maria hadn't listened to Juan? What if she had stuck her finger in the outlet? She could've gotten badly hurt and would have regretted that decision for the rest of her life.

What happens when we don't follow this "key" to the hermeneutics code—when we don't listen to and obey God and the Bible? In the end, we always get hurt in some way. We'll either get our feelings hurt, not be as close to God as we can be, or maybe even get hurt physically.

How can we listen and obey its words?

We can begin by reading them! We can't listen to and obey God if we aren't reading the letter He wrote to us. The Bible is one of the best ways we stay close to God, and we have to read it in order to hear from Him and know how to obey Him.

After reading it, we must act on what we read. Let's look at an example. In Ephesians 4:32, God tells us to:

Be kind to one another, tenderhearted, forgiving each other, just as God in Christ also has forgiven you.

Listening to and obeying this verse means we must be kind to each other, even if our

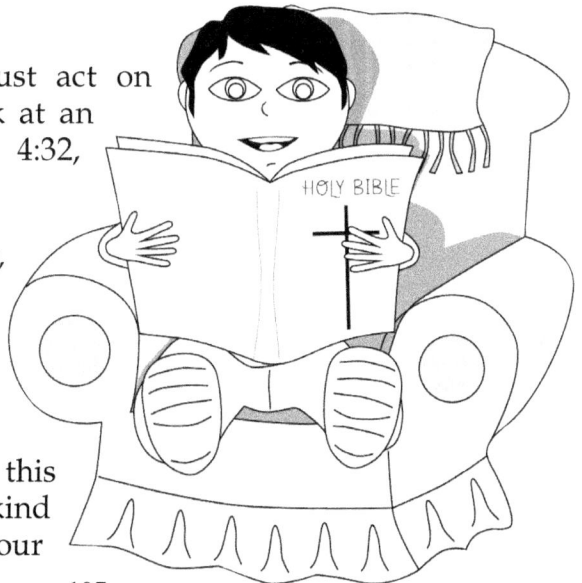

friends aren't being nice to us. We must also forgive each other. So, if one of your friends says something mean to you, God wants you to forgive him, even if you don't feel like it. Forgiving your friends shows that you are obeying God and acknowledging that He is the authority in your life.

If we are to understand the Bible correctly, we must remember that its words—God's words—are our authority. God is much smarter and wiser than we are, and He also wants what's best for us. He wants us to be joyful, but that happens only when we listen and obey the words He's given us in the Bible.

Make It YOURS!

- Why is God the best authority figure in the whole universe?

- Who's smarter—God or you?

- If we don't listen to and obey God and His Word, what happens?

14

Get the BIG-PICTURE

Congratulations! You are doing a great job, learning all the "cipher keys" we use to read and understand Scripture better! You've explored three keys so far and are filling your brain with all kinds of wonderful information about God and the Bible.

We're almost done! Now we'll explore the last key in this chapter. Keep up the good work!

The Big Picture

"Shhh!" Mr. Tulls whispered as he ushered his students into another room at the museum. "Sandy, Trisha, and Michael, move over here."

The students entered a side door into a huge room. The walls were like skyscrapers, and they could barely see the top.

As they entered the room, they found themselves walking on a ledge, almost like a bridge but inside. It was strange, but they were excited because they could look down and see that they were really high up!

The wall on their right had some kind of picture on it, and as they all gathered around one part, here's what they saw:

They saw two men—one holding a white container and the other holding a cup. Michael and Trisha furrowed their brows. What was so special about these two men? The children couldn't see much else because the wall was so big, and while it was interesting, they didn't understand who the men were, what they were doing, or what was so special about the picture. (They didn't understand its context!)

The class continued winding around on the ledge and made their way farther back until they entered a balcony. The balcony was dark and Mr. Tulls told them to move close to the window in front of them. The children complied and the museum guide told them all to be quiet, because they were going to witness something spectacular...

Suddenly the lights flashed on and Michael, Trisha, and all their classmates gasped at what they saw.

"Lunch atop a Skyscraper"
(Adapted from http://news.harvard.edu)

111

The picture of the two men was actually just one section of a huge picture that took up the entire wall! The only part they could see when they were close up was what was in the box.

"Wow," Michael said. "It's so strange that we could only see just a small part, but when we backed up, we could see the whole picture!"

"Definitely," Trisha agreed. "I guess we shouldn't be so quick to assume (think) that what we first see is all there is to see!"

"I've learned my lesson," Michael said. "This is so cool!"

Mr. Tulls' class learned an important lesson that day. Many times, what we see at first is not the whole picture. Because we are human and are small compared to the whole planet and universe, we can't always see the big picture. When we stand on the beach and look at the ocean, we see only a tiny fragment of how big the ocean really is.

We have a limited perspective, but sometimes when we back up we can see the full picture—or more of it than we could when we were close.

The Bible is a Picture... of Sorts

You have been doing great in our adventures learning about the Bible. You know by now that it is a book God gave us to tell us about Him and how we can know and love Him more.

We've also learned about certain tips we can use to "decode" the Bible—help us read and understand it better. The first is that it *means what it says* (the Literal, Grammatical, and Historical Method). We should always take the Bible seriously and do our best to find code-breaker #2—its *context*. We should constantly look for the W's of verses we read (*Who, What, When, Where, and Why*). The third cipher key is super-important because we must always remember that *God (and the Bible) is smarter than we are.* We are supposed to listen to and obey what God says because He knows what's best—even if we don't always agree.

Now we arrive at the last code-breaker…*the Bible is like a picture*. When we read one part of it, we have to remember the whole.

One main story runs throughout the entire Bible and makes it like one big picture even though we read only parts at a time. If you remember, that theme is called the gospel—the story of how God is rescuing us from our sin through His Son, Jesus Christ. God loves us so much that He decided to bring us together with Him again. This is possible only through accepting Jesus into our hearts because He made a way for us through His death, burial, and resurrection.

This story—the gospel—is what we must look for in every passage we read. Every single part of the Bible reveals the gospel in some way. So, when we read the Bible, we must remember to step back and remember that there's always more than the specific passage we are reading.

Who Cares?

Why is it important to "step back" and remember the theme of the Bible? Because if we don't, we'll miss out on the big picture! If we don't place each verse, passage, chapter, and book within the context of the gospel, we'll have an incomplete understanding of what God is trying to tell us.

An Example: Exodus

Though there are many fantastic passages in the Bible, a popular one is the story of Moses and how God used him to lead the Israelites out of Egypt.

It's fascinating to read about the plagues and how God worked in Pharaoh's heart to cause him to let the Israelites go (Exodus 4-14). Then God rescued the Israelites once and for all when He parted the sea and they walked through on dry land, but Pharaoh and his army were washed away when the waters came crashing down.

While this is a great story, it does not stand alone. We must look beyond this particular story to see 1) what it tells us about God, and 2) how it fits within the greater story of the Bible.

What it Tells us About God

What does this story tell us about God? A couple of things. First, we learn that God is all-powerful. The Pharaoh was the most powerful man in the world, yet God was much stronger and freed the Israelites from Pharaoh's grasp.

Second, God is faithful and gracious. He knew that His people (the Israelites) were slaves and heard their prayers to be free. A long time before that, God promised Abraham that He would make a great people out of Abraham's descendants (children, great-grandchildren, great-great-grandchildren, and so on). This story shows us how God was faithful to that promise and gracious in setting His people free from captivity.

Third, God is trustworthy. The Israelites had a problem with grumbling and complaining. When Moses talked with Pharaoh about letting the Israelites go, Pharaoh sometimes got angry and made the Israelites work harder. The Israelites responded by complaining and whining against God. They didn't trust Him; they didn't think He knew what He was doing.

At the end of the story, we discover that God definitely knows what He's doing and is worth putting our trust in. We can learn from Israel's mistake. Unlike them, we can trust God even when things don't go our way.

We can learn several more things about God from this story; but that's a good start.

How it Fits within the Big Picture

Now, how does this story fit in with the gospel—God's plan to save us from sin?

First, we see that God is faithful to His Word. He promised to save us through His Son Jesus, just as He promised to free Israel from Pharaoh in Egypt. He kept His promise! He freed Israel from Pharaoh, and He sent His Son Jesus to die on the cross for our sins so we can spend forever and ever with Him.

Second, the last plague (the firstborn son) foreshadows what Christ would do for us. The last plague came with a warning: God told everyone to cover their doorways with the blood of a lamb. They were to eat the lamb for dinner and place its blood on the top and sides of the door. If they obeyed, the angel of the Lord would pass over their home and would not kill the firstborn son. But if they disobeyed and didn't listen, their firstborn son would die.

The Israelites listened to and obeyed God; the Egyptians didn't. Pharaoh and all of Egypt woke up in the middle of the night to find their firstborn sons dead (Exodus 12:30).

This plague showed what Christ would do for us. Jesus came as the Lamb—He died in our place so we would be passed over—so our sins could be forgiven and we could go to heaven. The consequence for sin is death (Romans 6:23). Because we all sin, we all deserve to die and spend forever in hell apart from Jesus. But God didn't want that to happen, so He sent Jesus to die in our place.

That's the story of the gospel. Jesus came and took our place. But we have to accept His gift just as the Israelites had to listen and obey God's instructions. Christ's gift is free, just as God's instructions were free to the Israelites. It didn't cost them anything. But we have to accept it in order to be covered by Christ's blood like the Israelites were covered by the blood of the lamb.

Can you see how this story fits within the big picture of the Bible? God fills the Bible with lots of little stories that tell us about Him and help us understand the gospel better. The gospel is the big story, and every other story fits into it somehow.

Just as Michael and Trisha saw the little picture first and then stood back to see it within the context of the full picture, we can see every little part of the Bible in the context of its big story, the gospel. It's pretty exciting, isn't it?

This is one more reason to make sure we don't stop at reading just one section of the Bible. Reading one verse is good, but it will always give us a limited perspective of the Bible. Instead, we should read as much as we can because each verse contributes a piece of the bigger picture.

So, when we read the Bible, we need to remember to 1) look for what the passage tells us about God, and then 2) try to see how it fits within the big picture of the whole Bible—the gospel!

Make It YOURS!

- Why is it important to "step back" and remember the big story of the Bible?

- What two questions should we ask when we read any part of the Bible?

- The next time you read the Bible, try answering these two questions. It will help you understand it so much more!

15

The Finish Line

Have you ever been in a race? Maybe you run on a team or have competed in a track meet. If not, you have probably raced a friend or sibling down the street!

What is the best part of a race? If you are lucky enough to be the fastest, the best part is crossing the finish line. What a great feeling to run as fast as you can and cross the finish line out of breath but in first place!

You are about to cross a very big finish line, friends! In just a couple of pages, you will be finished reading this book, having learned many amazing truths about God and the Bible.

Congratulations!

Looking Back

One thing we're not supposed to do in a race is to look back. Looking back usually causes problems. We can trip, lose focus, or slow down without realizing it.

When in a race, we're always supposed to look forward and keep our attention on the finish line.

That works well for running races, but in this journey we've taken together, looking back is a good thing. When we look back at what we've learned, we are reminded of God's truths and can commit them to memory even better.

So before we cross the finish line of this book, let's take a couple of minutes to look back on the journey we're completing.

What the Bible Is

We began our adventure learning what the Bible is. First we discovered that it's *inerrant*, that it is absolutely perfect in every single way. There are zero mistakes in the Bible, which is impressive because it's a large book written over a long period of time.

Next we learned that it is *infallible*, that the Bible cannot lie or deceive us. The Bible is not only error-free, but it's also unable to make mistakes because God (Who is perfect), is its Author. A perfect God cannot write an imperfect book.

The third fact we learned about the Bible is that it's *inspired*—it's a present just for us. God used people to write down the words in the Bible, but He also told them exactly what to say. No paragraph, word, or letter written in the Bible is there by mistake. God told the human authors exactly what He wanted written in His book, and they obeyed completely.

We also learned that the Bible is *alive*. No, it doesn't breathe or move on its own, but God does use its words to teach us how to live and how to love Him each and every day. The Holy Spirit (who lives inside us if we have accepted Jesus) works with the words of the Bible to make us smarter and wiser and to help us live in ways that bring a smile to God's face.

The last fact we learned in Section One is that God's Word is a *story*. The Bible isn't a big book made up of a bunch of random writings. It is one big story that tells us the gospel—how God carried out His plan to save us through His Son, Jesus Christ.

How It Was Put Together

Once we finished learning what the Bible is, we turned our attention to how it was put together. First we discovered that the Bible is like a puzzle. Do you remember the story of Jimmy and

Lizzy from Chapter Six? They had quite the adventure, finding puzzle pieces and putting them together over a long time.

That's similar to how the Bible was put together. It was written one book at a time and was put together over a long period of time as each was written.

Next we learned that the Bible was not originally written in English. It was written in three languages: Hebrew, Greek and Aramaic. We looked at pictures of these languages and were impressed that we have the Bible in English at all today!

After that, we learned that the original manuscripts of the Bible had to be copied and translated into other languages so more people could read them. There are two ways to do this: translations and paraphrases. Translations are made up of word-for-words and thought-for-thoughts, and these stay as close to the original words as possible.

Paraphrases, on the other hand, move further away from the original words the Bible was written in. The people who paraphrase the Bible interpret it for us, which is nice, but we must be careful because they aren't always correct.

Not many people (even adults) know how the Bible was put together, so you added a bunch of wisdom to your brain when reading that section!

Your Faith

In Section Three, we paused to take a look at our personal relationships with Jesus. We saw that we can learn a whole lot about God and the Bible, but unless we have a relationship with Him (unless we invite Him into our hearts as Lord), we're not using what we know.

Do you remember Jeremy? His parents were excellent water skiers, and he knew everything about the sport, but he had never tried it himself. He was shocked to find that he wasn't very good at it once he tried! Knowing about something intellectually (in our brains) is not the same as knowing something experientially (personally, for ourselves).

Jeremy learned that his parents' skills were not enough to make him a skier. He had to do it for himself. In the same way, we have to make a decision to follow Jesus on our own. We cannot rely on our parents' faith to get us into heaven to spend forever with Jesus. We have to make that decision for ourselves.

Accepting Jesus in our hearts is the first step in allowing the Bible to become more than words in our lives. The Holy Spirit partners with us to teach us God's truths when we are His children, and there's no greater adventure in the whole world than that!

Breaking the "Code"

After learning what the Bible is, how it was put together and then pausing to see where we are in our faith, we moved to the final section — how to read the Bible.

We learned that the Bible has a "secret code" for reading and understanding it correctly. The key to this code is called hermeneutics, and it allows us to decipher the code all by ourselves.

The first key to the code is that the Bible *means what it says*. We must read the Bible literally and understand that it follows grammatical rules, like everything else we read. We can always take it seriously too, because it is true, not fiction. It is more accurate than our history books and helps us understand a lot more than our history books as well.

The second key to the code is the *W's* or *context*. Every time we read the Bible, we must ask who the passage is about and/or talking to, what is going on in the story, when the passage is taking place, where the story is happening, and why it's there. In other words, we need to understand context. A great tool to help us do this is a study Bible, and it would be a good idea to ask for one as a present if you don't already have one.

The third key to deciphering the Bible "code" is to remember that *God is smarter than we are...and so is His Word*. Sometimes we don't want to listen to or obey what God says. We think we know better than God, just like Maria thought she knew better than her big brother, Juan, about the electrical plug.

When we read the Bible, we must pay close attention to what it says and trust that God knows what He is talking about. He is much smarter, wiser, bigger, and way more powerful than we can even understand. He created us; and we can never be smarter than the One who made us!

We must listen to Him and obey Him, otherwise we could get hurt and not live as fully or as well as we can if we obey Him.

The final key to hermeneutics is focusing on *getting the big picture*. Mr. Tulls' class learned a valuable lesson about this at the museum. Most of what we see or read in the Bible is just a small part of all that is there. Just as Trisha and Michael could see only a small section of the photograph until they moved back, we see only a small section of the big picture of the Bible when we read a passage.

So when we read stories like Moses and the Exodus, we should constantly look for two things: 1) what does the passage/story tell us about God, and 2) how does the story reveal the big story of the gospel?

Though answering those two questions will take practice, it will always help us keep the big picture (the gospel) in mind when we read the smaller stories of the Bible.

You, friend, have just crossed the finish line, and you are a winner! I am so proud of you! You have learned so much about God and the Bible, your brain must be exhausted! Mine is for sure!

I pray that as you move forward in your life and faith in Jesus, you will always look back and remember what you've learned. God loves you and is celebrating with you!

He wants you to continue learning as much as you can about Him through His Word and has many wonderful plans for your life. Keep seeking Him and asking Him to reveal Himself to you through the Bible. Have fun on your journey with Him from this point forward!

Lots Of Thanks!

Nothing of eternal value is ever accomplished alone. God decided to make us creatures of community, which was brilliant. Without a strong community of family and friends surrounding me through this project, this book simply would not exist.

After God—the only One Who deserves all credit and glory—my husband, Sean, is my rock. God knew what He was doing when He gave you to me, Love. Life in Him became vibrant and liberating when I met you, and it's a journey I eagerly embrace every day.

Marlene Dean, you are the true rock star with this one. Thank you so much for letting me soak up your wisdom, advice, and insight throughout this process. God has gifted you with enormous talent and an acute ability to reach the minds and hearts of children. If children learn anything through this book, it will be because of you.

To my other contributors – Dr. Towns, Pastor Jeff Cranston, Pastor Brooks Cail, Pastor Marvin Suitt, Pastor Brian Moore, Carie Cash, Belinda Furby, Kaci Hollingsworth, Sherry Goebel, Tina Modugno—our phenomenal illustrator, and Christina Miller, the editor straight from heaven….. your insight astounds me. Thanks for letting me draw from the depths of your wisdom and talent.

And to the rest of my family and friends in Jesus, thank you for your constant prayers, encouragement, and support. I dearly wish I could write a book of thanks for each of you, but know your kindness is being recorded in heaven, where it matters.

Let the adventure in Him continue!

Mindifofuuly

Mindi Jo Furby

www.ingramcontent.com/pod-product-compliance
Lightning Source LLC
LaVergne TN
LVHW021350080426
835508LV00020B/2200